A NATURALIST'S

MAMMALS
OF
SRI LANKA

Gehan de Silva Wijeyeratne

JOHN BEAUFOY PUBLISHING

First published in the United Kingdom in 2020 by John Beaufoy Publishing,
11 Blenheim Court, 316 Woodstock Road, Oxford OX2 7NS, England
www.johnbeaufoy.com

10 9 8 7 6 5 4 3 2 1

Photo Captions and credits
Front cover: *main image* Leopard © Senal Siriwardene *bottom left* Elephant © Senal Siriwardene *bottom centre* Striped
Dolphin © Gehan de Silva Wijeyeratne; *bottom right* Sloth Bear © Rajiv Welikala.
Back cover: Indian Grey Mongoose © Namal Kamalgoda
Title page: Elephants at Minneriya © Gehan de Silva Wijeyeratne. **Contents page:** Purple-faced Leaf Monkey © Rajiv
Welikala.
Main descriptions: photos are denoted by a page number followed by t (top), c (centre), b (bottom), l (left) or r (right).
All photos are by Gehan de Silva Wijeyeratne except:
Chamara Amarasinghe 57, 62b, 63tr, 66t, 69; **Charles Anderson** 144, 157, 159br; **Melody Baran courtesy NOAA
Fisheries** 142bl, 142br; **Lillia Bernedette** 20bl; **Neville Buck** 95tl, 96bl; **Riaz Cader** 96br, 130tr; **Pierre de Chabannes**
21bl; **Rohit Chakravarty** 78, 82t, 82b, 87b; **Rajith Dissanayake** 25b; **David Element** 38; **Brock Fenton** 70tl, 75tl,
77b, 84tl, 84tc; **Sampath de A Goonatilake** 8, 8, 33, 34t, 35bl, 36t, 36b, 42b; **Andrew Griffin** 130tl, 130b; **Kithsiri
Gunawardena** 9, 20bc, 71br, 74b, 85b, 102t, 104; **Timothy Hornby** 59br, 75tr, 86tl, 86tr, 86b; **Chitral Jayatilake**
94b, 95b, 117t, 124bl; **Chandima Jayaweera** 90; Thomas A Jefferson/VIVA Vaquita 163; **Namal Kamalgoda** 8, 8 25t,
93br, 102b, 103, 105, 107br; **Tharaka Kusuminda** 27t, 29t, 42t, 56t, 58t, 61bl, 62tl, 63tl, 63bl, 63bc, 63br, 64tr, 68tl,
68tr, 68b, 70tr, 70b, 71bl, 72, 73t, 73b, 74t, 75b, 76l, 76r, 77tl, 77tr, 79t, 89tl, 89tr, 89bl, 80tl, 80tr, 81t, 81b, 83t, 83b,
84b, 85tl, 85tr, 87t, 88b; **Tasso Leventis** 15, 162b; **Burton Lim** 56b, 60t, 61br, 65tl, 65bl, 65br, 67t, 71c, 89br, 84tr, 88t;
Vincent Luk 64b, 80b; **Clive Martin** 142t, 143br, 160t; **Suyama Meegaskumbura** 9, 9, 35tr, 37, 40, 46, 47, 48b, 50, 51t,
51b, 52, 53; **Sanjay Molur** 32, 34bl, 34br; **Ranil Nanayakkara** 9, 9, 29b, 35tl, 35br, 48t, 54, 60b, 64tl, 66b, 67b, 71tr,
79b; **Paula Olson** 143bl, 143tr; **Paula Olson courtesy Institute of Marine Science** 136b, 136c, 136t; **Paula Olson
courtesy International Whaling Commission** 135t, 137tr, 138br, 141, 150t, 161t; **Paula Olson courtesy Pacific Islands
Fisheries Science Center** 145bl, 145tl, 145tr, 146b, 146t, 149b, 149tl, 150b, 151b, 151t, 152t, 154b, 154t; **Paula Olson
courtesy Southeast Fisheries Science Center** 133, 134, 149tr, 152cr, 161b; **Paula Olson courtesy Southwest Fisheries
Science Center** 135b, 137br, 148t, 152b, 152cl, 153c, 156c, 158, 159t; **Vardhan Patankar** 127, 128t, 128c, 128b;
Kaushal Patel 62tr; **Gehan Rajeev** 27b; **Shutterstock/ASIRI** 62 129; **Ruchira Somaweera** 20br; **Christian Stepf** 96t,
113b; **Andrew Sutton** 132br, 140cl, 140cr, 147, 148b, 153t, 153b, 156t, 156bl, 156br, 162t; **Nadeera Weerasinghe** 9,
118b; **Rajiv Welikala** 24bl, 93bl, 112b; **Wildlife Heritage Trust (WHT)** 9, 9, 9, 39, 41, 49; **Nilushan Wijesinghe** 17,
59bl; **Wildlife Conservation Society Galle** 8, 20tl, 65tr, 91, 121br; **Nayaer Youakim** 95tr, 113t, 114.

ISBN 978-1-912081-44-8

Edited by Krystyna Mayer
Designed by Alpana Khare Graphic Design
Printed and bound in Malaysia by Times Offset (M) Sdn. Bhd.

·CONTENTS·

Introduction

For an Asian destination, Sri Lanka is a surprisingly easy place in which to see mammals. This is because although the absolute number of species is much less than in, say, mainland India, the species density per square kilometre is extraordinarily high. In India, you would need to be in the core zone of Corbett National Park to see anything close to the number of species encountered in Sri Lanka on a good game drive in a national park like Yala. This compact photographic guide covers just over 90 per cent of all mammals recorded in Sri Lanka and is ideal for a field trip.

Topography & Climatic Zones

Sri Lanka's topography features lowlands along the coast, which give rise within a short distance to the central hills that rise above 2,400m in altitude. The island can be divided into three peneplains, or steps, first described by the Canadian scientist Adams in 1972. The lowest peneplain is 0–30m, the second rises to 480m and the third to 1,800m.

Sri Lanka can be broadly divided into three regions (hill zone, low country wet zone and dry zone) resulting from the interactions of rainfall and topography. Rainfall is affected by monsoonal changes that bring rain during two seasons, namely the south-west monsoon (May–August) and north-east monsoon (October–January). Their precipitation is heavily influenced by the central hills – the monsoons deposit rain across the country and contribute to the demarcation of climatic regimes.

The humid, lowland wet zone in the south-west does not show marked seasons, being fed by both the south-west and north-east monsoons. The low country wet zone receives 200–500cm of rain from the south-west monsoon and afternoon showers from the north-east monsoon. Humidity is high, rarely dropping below 97 per cent, while temperatures are 27–31° C over the year.

The mountainous interior lies in the wet zone and rises to more than 2,400m. Rainfall is generally well distributed, except in Uva Province, which gets very little rainfall in June–September. Temperatures are cooler in the lowlands, varying from being chilly in the mornings to warm by noon. In the mid-elevations such as the area around Kandy, the temperature varies between 17° C and 31° C during the year. Temperature variations during a 24-hour cycle will, however, be far less varied. The mountains are cooler, within a band of 14–32° C during the year. There may be frost in the higher hills in December and January, when night-time temperatures fall below zero.

The rest of the country, three-quarters of Sri Lanka's land area, consists of the dry zone of the northern, southern and eastern plains. These

Riverine Forest in Wilpattu National Park

regions receive 60–190cm of rain each year, mainly from the north-east monsoon. The dry zone is further divided into the arid zones of the north-west and south-east, which receive less than 60cm of rain as they are not in the direct path of the monsoonal rains.

TIME TO TRAVEL

Because of the climatic variation, some parts of the country are usually dry and enjoying good weather. Generally speaking, Sri Lanka is a year-round destination for wildlife enthusiasts and photographers. January–April marks the warm, dry season in the lowlands and is the favoured time for visitors as it coincides with the northern winter. In the highlands at Nuwara Eliya and Horton Plains, for example, in sharp contrast, frost may be experienced in January–February. The inter-monsoonal lull is in February–April. February is the driest in the south-west. The best time for visiting birdwatchers extends from November to April, with February being a good month as it is largely free of rain. During this period, migrants are present, adding to the tally of birds. Wildlife viewing in the national parks in the dry zone is best during dry, hot and dusty times, when animals are concentrated around waterholes, with streams reduced to a mere trickle.

CLASSIFICATION & MAMMALS

Biologists group all living things into various taxonomic levels or ranks, increasing in granularity as one goes deeper into the levels. One of the lower levels comprises classes such as birds or mammals. The mammal class (Mammalia) is in turn broken down into orders and families. Examples of mammal orders in Sri Lanka include the Insectivora (shrews), Chiroptera (bats), and Carnivora. Orders, in turn, consist of related families. For example, the Carnivora includes the Canidae (dog family with jackals, wolves and so on.), Felidae (cats), Herpestidae (mongooses), Mustelidae (otters, weasels), Ursidae (bears) and Viverridae (civets, palm civets).

Within a family animals are grouped into genera and given a specific epithet. The Golden Jackal is thus *Canis aureus*, while the Black-backed Jackal is *C. mesomelas*. Latin (scientific) names may change from time to time as taxonomists revise their opinions on an animal's relationship to others. However, they are often more stable and more reliable in deducing which species is being referred to than common names. For example, what was referred to as the Black-backed Jackal in Sri Lanka is actually the widespread Golden Jackal *C. aureus*. The form found in Sri Lanka does have a pronounced black

The Golden Jackal is best seen in dry zone national parks

back. Taxonomists sometimes use a trinomial with the usual binomial name to indicate a subspecies, or geographical race. The Golden Jackal found in Sri Lanka then becomes *C. a. naria*. To summarize, the Golden Jackal is classified as follows.

Kingdom	Animalia
Phylum	Chordata
Subphylum	Vertebrata
Class	Mammalia
Order	Carnivora
Family	Canidae
Genus	*Canis*

Taxonomy remains fluid and poses issues for scientists and beginners alike. Your understanding of the behaviour of mammals will grow better if you attempt to understand family traits.

What is a Mammal?

Certain attributes define mammals. They all have hair on the skin, feed their young with milk and, with the exception of the Echidna and Duck-billed Platypus (which lay eggs), give birth to live young. Mammals also generally have four external limbs that in the case of marine mammals like whales and dolphins may be modified into flippers and in others may be reduced to vestiges. All mammals take oxygen directly from the air, which is why marine mammals have to surface to breathe and exhale. If whales and dolphins are trapped in fishing nets and cannot come up for air, they drown. Mammals also have a heart and a blood circulatory system that allows them to maintain a constant body temperature. They can cool themselves by using sweat glands that help cool the body by evaporation. The ability of mammals to retain a stable temperature is one of the reasons why they have been able to colonize a variety of habitats, from deserts to the ice packs of the Arctic and Antarctic. The same holds true for birds.

Yala National Park has many man-made water holes

Mammal Watching in Sri Lanka

Mammals are most easily seen in dry zone national parks such as Yala, Bundala, Uda Walawe, Wasgomuwa and Wilpattu, with Yala ranking as the best place to see them. Some species, such as the Grey Mongoose, which is very common in the north-central province, become very rare in the south. Therefore even for mammals of dry lowlands, taking in a mix of parks in the north-central province and the deep south helps increase the species diversity. The endemic primates, such as the Purple-faced Leaf Monkey and Toque Macaque, can be found at certain sites. Talangama Wetland in the suburbs of Colombo is good for the Critically Endangered western subspecies of the Purple-faced Leaf Monkey, but is also surprisingly rich in other mammals. However, due to the human population density, many of the mammals are nocturnal. Colombo is a wetland city and now has at least three good sites for wildlife enthusiasts. Because its wetlands are connected by a system of drainage and irrigation canals, it provides a connectivity for animals like Fishing Cats,

Talangama Wetland

which are found in good numbers. However, they are very wary and not easy to see.

Visiting a lowland rainforest such as Sinharaja or Kithulgala is essential to pick up some wet zone species, as well as to see subspecies like the Giant Squirrel, Purple-faced Leaf Monkey and Toque Macaque. The endemic Layard's Palm Squirrel and endemic Sri Lanka Dusky-striped Squirrel extend up to the highlands. A highland site such as Horton Plains holds endemic small mammals, but these will only be seen by researchers who are laying small mammal traps. Although no new species are added if you visit sites such as Sinharaja and Kithulgala, the highlands nevertheless contain interesting montane forms of mammal such as primates. Hakgala Botanical Gardens is excellent for the highland subspecies of the Toque Macaque, and the 'Bear Monkey' subspecies of the Purple-faced Leaf Monkey. Both are distinctive subspecies worth seeing.

Cultural sites such as Sigirya and Polonnaruwa are very good for mammals, especially primates. I have on many occasions enjoyed taking a game drive around the Sigiriya rock alongside the moat. My game drives regularly produce the Grey Mongoose, Toque Macaque, Hanuman Langur, the northern subspecies of the Purple-faced Leaf Monkey, Indian Palm Squirrel, Giant Squirrel and others. In the evenings I have encountered elephants, Grey Slender Lorises, Golden Palm Civets and Golden Jackals.

ENDEMIC MAMMALS

The following 22 mammals are endemic to Sri Lanka. In my previous articles and books, I noted that 18 species are endemic. There are now four new endemics, brought about by the elevation of the Sri Lanka Dusky-striped Squirrel *Funambulus sublineatus*, and the split of the Golden Palm Civet *Paradoxurus zeylonensis*, an endemic, into three endemic species – the Wet-zone Golden Palm Civet *P. aureus*, Montane Golden Palm Civet *P. montanus* and Dry-zone Golden Palm Civet *P. stenocephalus*. The Highland Shrew *Suncus montanus* has been split from *S. niger* in India, with each species an endemic in Sri Lanka and India respectively.

PRIMATES

Lorises (Lorisidae)   **Monkeys (Cercopithecidae)**

Red Slender Loris
Loris tardigradus

Toque Macaque
Macaca sinica

Hanuman Langur
Semnopithecus priam

RODENTIA

Squirrels (Sciuridae)

Layard's Palm Squirrel *Funambulus layardi*

Sri Lanka Dusky-striped Squirrel
Funambulus obscurus

Rats & Mice (Muridae)

Sri Lanka Spiny Mouse *Mus fernandoni*

Sri Lanka Bi-coloured Spiny Mouse
Mus mayori

Montane Rat
Rattus montanus

Ohiya Rat
Srilankamys ohiensis

Long-tailed Climbing
Mouse *Vandeleuria nolthenii*

SORICOMORPHA

Shrews (Soricidae)

Sri Lanka Long-tailed Shrew
Crocidura miya

Sinharaja Shrew
Crocidura hikmiya

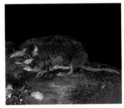

Kelaart's Long-clawed Shrew
Feroculus feroculus

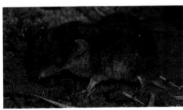

Pearson's Long-clawed Shrew *Solisorex pearsoni*

Highland Shrew *Suncus montanus*

Sri Lanka Pygmy Shrew
Suncus fellowesgordoni

Sri Lanka Shrew
Suncus zeylanicus

CARNIVORA
Civets (Viverridae)

Wet-zone Golden Palm Civet
Paradoxurus aureus

Dry-zone Golden Palm Civet
Paradoxurus stenocephalus

Montane Golden Palm Civet
Paradoxurus montanus

ARTIODACTYLA
Chevrotain (Tragulidae)

White-spotted Mouse-deer *Tragulus meminna*

Yellow-striped Mouse-deer *Tragulus kathygre*

Visitors have a high likelihood of seeing the two diurnal primates and the Layard's Palm Squirrel. Sadly many of the endemics are small nocturnal mammals that are seldom seen other than by specialists.

Key Sites for Terrestrial Mammals & Other Wildlife

TALANGAMA WETLAND

This wetland on the outskirts of Colombo is traversed by motorable roads, which make access easy for wildlife enthusiasts. The complex of ponds, canals and paddy fields makes it a rich and varied wetland site. The main target mammal here is the endemic Critically Endangered western subspecies of the Purple-faced Leaf Monkey. The wetland still holds the Fishing Cat, Small Indian and Common Palm Civets, Indian Hare and Crested Porcupine, which are all almost entirely nocturnal. During day the Brown Mongoose is a possibility.

Although not good for seeing mammals by day, for general wetland wildlife, the Diyasaru Wetland Park and Beddegana Wetland in Colombo's suburbs are worth a visit. Entry to the park is by ticket.

WASGOMUWA NATIONAL PARK

Located south of Polonnaruwa and north of the Knuckles Range and Matale foothills, Wasgomuwa consists of riverine gallery forest along the Mahaweli and dry monsoon forest in the low foothills. Mammals here include elephants, leopards, Sloth Bears, Golden Jackals, Spotted Deer, Sambar, mongooses and civets, as well as the Slender Loris and Hanuman Langur. Along with Yala and Uda Walawe, this is one of the best year-round parks for elephants. It is reported to have a high density of Sloth Bears, but they are very difficult to see.

HORTON PLAINS NATIONAL PARK

Sri Lanka's second and third highest peaks, Kirigalpotta (2,395m) and Thotupola Kanda (2,357m) are found here. Three important rivers, the Mahaweli, Kelani and Walawe, originate in Horton Plains. The highlight for walkers is World's End or Baker's Falls.

Numbers of Sambar, the island's largest deer, have soared in the last decade, with a corresponding increase in their main predator, the leopard. I have seen leopards here, and there have been accounts of leopards stalking Sambar in full view of people having a picnic lunch. Other mammals include the Wild Boar, Sri Lanka Dusky-striped Squirrel and highland subspecies of the Grizzled Indian Squirrel, Layard's Palm Squirrel, Toque Macaque and Bear Monkey (the montane subspecies of the Purple-faced Leaf Monkey). The nearest town is Nuwara Eliya, with a range of accommodation.

Horton Plains

Elephants in Uda Walawe National Park

UDA WALAWE NATIONAL PARK

This is probably the only park in Asia where a sighting of wild elephants can be guaranteed. In fact, elephants patiently wait inside the park's electric fence to be fed sugar cane by visitors passing by on the main road that borders the park. It is a mixture of abandoned Teak plantations, grassland, scrub jungle and riverine 'gallery forest' along the Walawe Ganga and Mau Ara. The elephants cluster in tightly knit family groups of up to four generations of related adult and subadult females and young. Other mammals include the Toque Macaque, Hanuman Langur, Spotted Deer, Wild Pig, Black-naped or Indian Hare and Ruddy Mongoose, as well as Jungle Cats seen in the evenings.

YALA (RUHUNU) NATIONAL PARK

Yala is Sri Lanka's most visited national park and the best in Sri Lanka for viewing a wide diversity of animals. It is a wonderful place with a spectrum of habitats, from scrub jungle, lakes and brackish lagoons to riverine areas. The park is divided into five blocks, of which Block 1 (Yala West) is the most visited. In some years, Yala may be closed on certain dates in September and October, when it is very dry. The biggest draws here are elephants, Sloth Bears and leopards – the park has one of the world's highest densities of leopards. About 40km beyond Hambantota on the A2, Tissamaharama has a broad range of accommodation. Near Block 1 of the park, top-end options include Cinnamon Yala, Jetwing Yala, Jetwing Safari Camp Yala and Wild Coast. These properties can also be used as bases for visiting Yala Block 5, which has motorable roads and was opened fairly recently. However, the accommodation at Kataragama is much closer to Block 5.

SINHARAJA

The Sinharaja Man and Biosphere Reserve was declared a World Heritage Site in 1988. It is arguably the most important biodiversity site in Sri Lanka, and internationally important for tropical biodiversity. Sinharaja comprises lowland and submontane wet evergreen forests with submontane Patana grassland in the east. A staggering 64 per cent of the tree species are endemic to Sri Lanka. The lower slopes and valleys have remnant *Dipterocarpus* forest, with the middle and higher slopes characterized by *Mesua* genus trees. Half of Sri Lanka's endemic mammals and butterflies are found here. Mammals visitors are most likely to see are the Purple-faced Leaf Monkey, Grizzled Indian or Giant Squirrel, Sri Lanka Dusky-striped Squirrel and Layard's Palm Squirrel; Toque Macaques are occasionally seen. Serious naturalists can stay at Martin's and Blue Magpie Lodge, near the reserve.

KUMANA NATIONAL PARK

Kumana adjoins Yala but access is from the east. Most visitors drive in from Pottuvil and Arugam Bay, about an hour away. The park has many waterbodies and is also a Ramsar Site. The character of the park is different although it is contiguous with the more heavily visited Yala Block 1. The mammals are similar to those in Yala.

LAHUGALA NATIONAL PARK

This is another park in the east of the island that is visited by people staying at Pottuvil and Arugam Bay. Elephants are the easiest to see. The forest is intermediate zone in character and has many wonderful old trees. The Satinwood Trees ('*Burutha*' in Sinhalese) are the most beautiful examples I have seen of this species on the island.

WHALE WATCHING

In May 2008, I broke the story that Sri Lanka is the best place in the world to see Blue Whales, based on sailing from Mirissa in southern Sri Lanka. Over a decade on, this still holds true. There is also the chance (albeit a low one) of seeing both Blue and Sperm Whales on the same sailing.

There are three key locations for whale watching in Sri Lanka – Mirissa, Trincomalee and Kalpitiya – and all are characterized by the presence of deep water close to shore. The development of Kalpitiya for whale watching began in February 2010, although it had become known for its Spinner Dolphins by 2009. The story that I broke that it may be one of Sri Lanka's top whale-watching sites was corroborated by seismic exploration data that became available in January 2010. I explained that the continental shelf was closer than had been depicted in the admiralty charts.

On a dedicated whale-watching tour that includes 5–7 sailings, it is possible to see 5–6 species. Twenty-nine or 30 species of cetacean (whales and dolphins) have been reported from Sri Lanka, depending on the book referred to. However, the inclusion of two, the Fin Whale and Northern Minke Whale, is considered doubtful. In the checklist for this book I have excluded the Fin Whale as there is a consensus that previous records may have been mistaken. The Dugong (order Sirenia) is very rare. There is one record of a juvenile Southern Elephant Seal. In the checklist, which retains the Minke Whale, the number of marine mammals adds up to 31 species. A more detailed account of whale-watching locations is available in *Wild Sri Lanka* (see p. 170).

Mirissa is the main hub for whale watching

ANATOMY

With bats and cetaceans (whales and dolphins), as is the case with birds, it helps to become familiar with what are known as topographical terms. These terms are a sort of linguistic shorthand to allow the species descriptions to be more concise and also to help people in the field to point out features. Learning the terms also helps you to become a better observer as the eye finds it easier to see things for which the brain has the words.

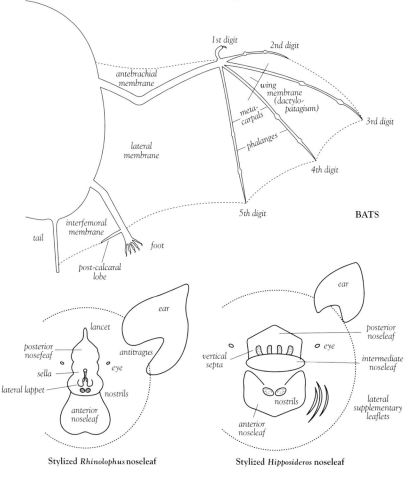

Stylized *Rhinolophus* noseleaf

Stylized *Hipposideros* noseleaf

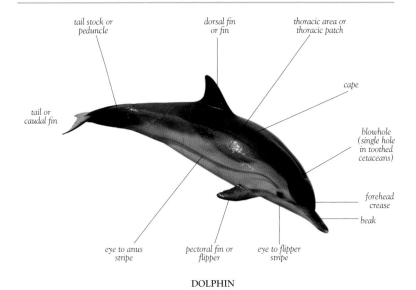

tail stock or peduncle

dorsal fin or fin

thoracic area or thoracic patch

cape

tail or caudal fin

blowhole (single hole in toothed cetaceans)

forehead crease

beak

eye to anus stripe

pectoral fin or flipper

eye to flipper stripe

DOLPHIN

GLOSSARY

Arboreal Tending to inhabit canopy of trees.

Cape In whales and dolphins refers to contrasting area of colour on upper surface near head that looks like a cape (or shawl) drawn over shoulders.

Crepuscular Active at dawn and dusk.

Diurnal Active by day.

Dorsal On upperparts of body. On mammals, dorsal stripes, for example, would refer to stripes running along back.

HBL Head and body length.

Nocturnal Active at night.

Pectorals Pectoral fins or flippers, positioned on sides and behind head. Long white flippers in a Humpback Whale are pectorals. Corresponds to front limbs of other mammals (arms in primates).

Pedicles Bony growths on skull that support growth of antlers.

Pod Social group of whales or dolphins.

Premaxillae (singular **premaxilla**) Skull bones that carry incisors.

Rut Period when deer are in season and males challenge other males for dominance to gain access to females.

Thoracic panel Sides of cetaceans may have contrasting patch of colour on sides of throat.

Ventral On undersurface.

LAND MAMMALS

Following some introductory text, the species descriptions are generally organized under habitat, distribution, behaviour and diet. Occasionally, headings are provided for subspecies (in Sri Lanka only) and 'where to see' details. Some mammals may be widespread, with a number of distinct subspecies (or races). In the late 1990s, efforts led by Rohan Pethiyagoda and his team at the Wildlife Heritage Trust saw a renaissance in Sri Lankan natural history exploration, and more than 100 new vertebrate species have been described to science. Pethiyagoda's efforts have inspired a new generation of naturalists to engage in describing new species.

ELEPHANTIDAE (ELEPHANTS)

Elephants are one of the six orders of hoofed mammal, although their hooves are more like toenails. The order Proboscidea (named in reference to the nose or proboscis) comprises only the Elephantidae family, with two genera and three species. African Savanna and African Forest Elephants, treated by some as a distinct species, are in the genus *Loxodonta*. The Asian Elephant is in the genus *Elephas*. Elephants are highly intelligent, long-lived mammals distinguished by an incredible nose, which also functions as a limb, one of the most sensitive organs in mammals. African Elephants have large ears and both sexes bear tusks, but only male Asian Elephants bear tusks. There are three Asian Elephant subspecies, and it is found in 13 countries. In evolutionary terms elephants are closest to the hyraxes (family Procaviidae), which are confined to Africa and the Middle East.

Asian Elephant ▪ *Elephas maximus*

Distinguished from the African Elephant by concave rather than convex back, and is also smaller. African has large, triangular ears, compared to smaller, rounded ears of Asian. Tip of trunk in Asian has one protuberance, or 'finger' (two in African). Asian is a forest elephant, while African is adapted to savannah. African uses its ears as an air-conditioning unit, while Asian, with a much lower tolerance to heat, is unlikely to emerge on to open grassland before the cool of the evening. In Asian only males carry tusks (in African, both sexes do so), which are elongated incisors. In African every individual grows tusks, but in Asian only a small proportion of males do so. In Sri Lanka it is estimated that only 7–8 per cent of males carry tusks. **DISTRIBUTION** Only a couple of hundred years ago, elephants ranged from scrub forests and grassland of dry lowlands to cloud forests of Horton Plains. Now, only a few pocketed groups remain in mid-hills around Peak Wilderness. Significant numbers of elephants remain only in dry lowlands. **BEHAVIOUR** Basic unit of elephant society is mother and calf. Bond group of elephants usually consists of related animals with subadult male siblings, female siblings, mothers, aunts and cousins. Adult female will suckle a calf that is not its own, and is termed an allomother. Bull elephants periodically undergo a biochemical change known as musth, when they are in peak breeding condition and are pumped up with hormonal secretions in their circulatory system. They are markedly more aggressive and a larger bull not in musth will give way to a smaller bull in musth. Radio-collaring studies by Dr Prithiviraj Fernando have shown that adult bulls may range over as much as 140km². Human-elephant conflict has escalated tremendously in recent years, and every year people and elephants are killed. Elephants face a grim future in Sri Lanka unless policy makers strive to keep open vast areas for wildlife to roam. **DIET** Needs combination of grassland on which to graze, and leaves from shrubs and trees to browse. **WHERE TO SEE** In Uda Walawe National Park, elephants are guaranteed, and Wasgomuwa National Park and Yala (Ruhuna) National Park are also good places for elephants. 'The Gathering' at Minneriya and Kaudulla National Parks is not to be missed in August–September.

Only male Asian Elephants develop tusks

The Elephant Gathering

The largest annually recurring gathering of elephants takes place in Sri Lanka. In Africa, large gatherings can also take place driven by years of drought, but they do not recur every year and their occurrence is too unpredictable for them to become a tourist attraction.

Each year, 'The Elephant Gathering' takes place on the receding shores of the Minneriya Lake (and Kaudulla Lake, which, as the crow flies, is a few kilometres away), in the north-central province. The Elephant Gathering at Minneriya provides a wonderful opportunity to watch the social dynamics of elephants. Clans of related elephants coalesce into herds when they converge on to Minneriya in a common quest for food, water, cover and mates. Smaller herds group into even larger ones, sometimes numbering more than 100 elephants. Adult bulls mix freely, using their trunks to test the air for adult females that are receptive. Bulls tussle for dominance and calves play with each other.

For more information see *Wild Sri Lanka* (p. 170) and my blog wildlifewithgehan. blogspot.com, 'Branding The Elephant Gathering – How It Came About'.

PRIMATES

The order Primates comprises 16 families, divided into two suborders. The Strepsirrhini comprises seven families (four families of lemur, aye-aye, galago and loris). The Haplorihini comprises nine families (tarsiers, marmosets, squirrel monkeys, capuchins, night monkeys, titis, howlers, Old World monkeys, gibbons and great apes). The Old World monkeys in the family *Cercopithecidae* are further divided into two subfamilies, the Cercopithecinae, which includes the baboons, macaques, guenons and others, and the Colobinae, containing the langurs and colobus species.

The suborder Prosimii (with the lorises), and the suborder Haplorhini containing the subfamilies Cercopithecinae and Colobinae, are represented in Sri Lanka. Although there are only five species, these span the primate evolutionary tree; three are diurnal and two are nocturnal. The ease with which primates can be seen makes Sri Lanka a very good location for primate studies. A study by Dr Wolfgang Dittus on the Toque Macaques is one of the longest running field studies in the world, spanning more than four decades.

The Prosimii are considered the most ancient suborder of the primates. In Sri Lanka it was believed until near the end of the twentieth century that only one species, the Grey Slender Loris *Loris lydekkerianus* was present. However, the loris found in the wet zone is distinctive, and was split into a new species, the Red Slender Loris *L. tardigradus*. The highland subspecies found in Horton Plains National Park and the isolated population in the Knuckles Range are potential candidates for a split. The montane subspecies went undetected for more than seven decades before a three-day search by primatologist Professor Anna Nekaris found it again in Horton Plains. Primates are among the best studied of Sri Lankan mammals thanks to Dr Wolfgang Dittus, Professor Nekaris, Dr Jinie Dela and their students.

LORISIDAE (LORISES)

The Lorisidae comprises two subfamilies: the Lorisinae with the lorises found in Asia, and the subfamily Perodictinae with the angwantibos and pottos found in Africa. The subfamily Lorisinae has two genera – *Loris* with two species and *Nycticebus* (slow lorises) with five species. The latter are confined to Southeast Asia and the Sunda Islands. The Grey Slender Loris is shared with India and the Red Slender Loris is endemic to Sri Lanka. The word loris may have arisen from the Dutch word *loeris* for clown.

Red Slender Loris ■ *Loris tardigradus*

Smaller than the Grey Slender Loris (opposite). Relatively small ears and longer muzzle. Fur reddish in colour. Dark markings around eyes more circular (or semicircular) compared to ovular or teardrop-shaped markings on Grey. **HABITAT** Prefers primary or secondary rainforest. **DISTRIBUTION** Confined to forests in wet zone. Populations can survive in extensive areas of home gardens mixed with wooded patches. **BEHAVIOUR** Home range is 1.5–15ha, but unlikely to survive in very small fragments because it does not travel great distances, and vulnerable to cats and dogs in forests fragmented due to housing developments. Stalks prey and grabs it with lightning speed once within strike range. Appears more reluctant than Grey to travel along the ground, making trees connected by vines or overlapping branches important. Loss of habitat has eliminated it from near Colombo, although I have friends who still have lorises visiting their forested gardens beside Bolgoda Lake. **DIET** Feeds mainly on insects but also eats other small animals. In captivity has been recorded eating fruits. **SUBSPECIES** *L. t. tardigradus*: lowland wet zone. *L. t. nycticeboides*: more dense and woollier coat, shorter limbs and ears covered in fur. Confined to cloud forests in and around Horton Plains National Park. Further studies may show it to be a distinct species.

Circular eye markings

Reddish fur

Grey Slender Loris ■ *Loris lydekkerianus*

Two subspecies, and descriptions below are for the Northern Grey Slender Loris *L. l. nordicus* of dry lowlands. Greyish coat and yellow pigmentation on ears, eyelids and muzzle. Dark shapes around eyes oval-like or teardrop shaped. Bigger than the Red Slender Loris (opposite). **HABITAT** Prefers slightly wooded scrub forest with closed canopy in dry lowlands. Often seen at forest edges where it presumably benefits from edge effect and access to wider range of prey. Adapted to forest disturbance and fragmentation better than other animals as more likely to come down and scramble along the ground, at times across main roads, or along barbed wire fences, to cross from one forested patch to another. **DISTRIBUTION** Distributed widely in dry lowlands, but appears more abundant in north-central province, especially around sites such as Sigiriya and Polonnaruwa. Particularly high density in Mannar Island. Curiously, no firm sight records in Yala – but I have spoken to safari drivers who have seen it in Bundala and Debera Wewa. **BEHAVIOUR** Most frequent call a thin, drawn-out whistle (a few seconds long) that can be mistaken for an insect call. Other calls described as chitter and scream. In Polonnaruwa observed to sleep communally with as many as 11 individuals. **DIET** Primarily insectivorous but also seen eating other animals such as snails and lizards. **SUBSPECIES** *L. l. nordicus*: throughout dry lowlands. Yellow pigmentation on ears, eyelids and muzzle. Endemic to Sri Lanka. *L. l. grandis*: woollier coat and little yellow pigmentation. Slightly heavier. Found in central mountains extending from Kandy to Knuckles Wilderness in rainforests. Endemic to Sri Lanka. Animal found in Knuckles may turn out to be distinct species or subspecies. **WHERE TO SEE** Scrub forests around Sigiriya and Polonnaruwa. Loris watching is conducted by Jetwing Vil Uyana and Kandalama Arboretum in their respective premises.

Skinny limbs

Oval or tear-shaped eye markings

> ### CERCOPITHECIDAE (OLD WORLD MONKEYS)
> The Old World monkeys of Asia and Africa are divided into two subfamilies, the Colobinae and Cercopithecinae. The endemic Purple-faced Leaf Monkey *Semnopithecus vetulus* and Hanuman Langur *S. priam* are in the Colobinae. The endemic Toque Macaque is in the Cercopithecinae.

Toque Macaque ▪ *Macaca sinica*

Appears very common since it occurs in significant numbers where visitors gather, such as at Cultural Triangle sites, but this is in fact not the case. **HABITAT** Favours forest cover near waterbodies. Occurs near human habitation, but needs trees for roosting. **DISTRIBUTION** Three subspecies occupy forested habitats all over the island. **BEHAVIOUR** Complex social organizations. Dominant males (alpha males) monopolize matings with receptive females, which form stable matrilines, with females belonging to castes with different degrees of social status. **DIET** Omnivorous. Wide range of plant and animal matter. **SUBSPECIES** Colour and length of hairs radiating from cap (toque) used to distinguish subspecies – this is not always easy in the field between dry zone and wet lowland subspecies. Subspecies *M. s. sinica* found in dry lowlands. Tips of hairs radiating from cap pale buffy. Wet zone subspecies *M. s. aurifrons* generally darker, with reddish or yellowish tips to hairs on toque. Montane subspecies *M. s. opisthomelas* has long hairs radiating from cap, with tips straw coloured. Upperparts and sides lack reddish-brown of lowland subspecies **WHERE TO SEE** Dry zone subspecies at Anuradhapura, Polonnaruwa and Sigiriya. Wet zone subspecies at Udawattakele in Kandy. Montane subspecies best seen at Hakgala Botanical Gardens. Used to people in all these places and approaches them if it thinks they have food.

Forms stable matrilines

Montane subspecies

Hanuman Langur ■ *Semnopithecus priam*

(Tufted Grey Langur)

Graceful monkey with sinuous long tail. May be mistaken for the Purple-faced Leaf Monkey (p. 24), which also has dark face, but in Sri Lanka easily told apart from the leaf monkey by pointed bonnet on head. Leaf monkey also has more extensive white whiskers on chin and cheeks. Hanuman has a habit of holding tail gracefully aloft when walking. **HABITAT & DISTRIBUTION** Scrub and riverine forests in dry lowlands. **BEHAVIOUR** Can form large troops exceeding 50 individuals, but mostly in troops of under 20, with dominant male. Usually very shy other than at a few temples where it has got used to people. Unlike Toque Macaques (opposite), habituated langurs generally not aggressive towards people. Often found in company of Spotted Deer, which benefit from leaves and fruits dropped by langurs, which benefit from the extra pairs of eyes. I have photographed large males banding together to drive away jackals that were stalking their troop. If they see or smell a large predator like a leopard, the langurs put up a furious medley of barking calls. **DIET** Herbivorous. Narrow diet confined to tender leaves, fruits and similar.

Pointed bonnet on head

Associates with Spotted Deer

Holds tail aloft while walking

Purple-faced Leaf Monkey ■ *Presbytis vetulus*

Shy monkey never seeming to be quite at ease with people. Montane subspecies habituated to people at Hakgala Botanical Gardens, but never approaches them with the boldness of the Toque Macaque (p. 22). On the outskirts of Colombo, in Talangama Wetland and around Bolgoda Lake, almost daily visitors to people's gardens. Lack of education among architects to design with neighbouring wildlife in mind is a factor that brings conflict. In human habitation, uses roofs as aerial walkways to compensate for trees that have often been felled by people building homes, landing with a thud on a roof and destroying clay roof tiles, which lets in water during rains. Such aggravation can easily be avoided by using roofing sheets that are not easily damaged by monkeys. **HABITAT & DISTRIBUTION** Found widely throughout where tall forests occur. Absent from northern peninsula. **BEHAVIOUR** Generally in small family troops of up to 6–12 individuals. One troop in Talangama had up

Subspecies nestor

to 40 individuals, but this is unusual and most other troops in Talangama comprise about six individuals. Alpha male hierarchy is standard social structure, with several females and young in troop. Loose associations form between young males, which create bachelor troops, and may collaborate to topple dominant alpha male. **DIET** Largely folivorous (leaf eating), and will eat fruits. Habit of raiding mango, jak and coconuts creates conflict with some local people. **SUBSPECIES** Four subspecies described (ranges of three suggested by their names): Southern Purple-faced Leaf Monkey *S. v. vetulus*, Dry Zone Purple-faced Leaf Monkey *S. v. philbricki*, and Western Purple-faced Leaf Monkey *S. v. nestor*. The Bear Monkey *S. v. monticola*, found in highlands, is very woolly in appearance.

Pale morph

Subspecies nestor

SCUIRIDAE (SQUIRRELS)

The Scuiridae family is in the order Rodentia, which encompasses many other mammals that behaviourally and in terms of external appearances may not seem closely related. However, anatomical features such as dentition link them as rodents. There are about 200 Scuiridae species worldwide, except in the Arctic, Antarctic and Australia. Four diurnal squirrel species and two nocturnal flying squirrel species are found in Sri Lanka. All four diurnal squirrels are in the genus *Funambulus* and are marked with three stripes on the back. The squirrels are characterized by long, furry tails, and by vocalizations being an important part of their behavioural strategy. They have far-carrying alarm calls and maintain territories by calling loud from a high vantage point. All Sri Lankan diurnal squirrels have a tendency to follow flocks of birds. The sexes of the squirrels do not show pronounced differences in size.

Layard's Palm Squirrel

▪ *Funambulus layardi*

(Flame-striped Squirrel)

Dark squirrel, about the size of the Indian Palm Squirrel (p. 26). Often gives presence away with bird-like chittering call, but not quite as vocal as Indian. If good views are had, beautiful 'flame-stripe' on back can be seen. Three dorsal stripes, with middle one being widest and longest. **HABITAT** Keeps to tall forests in wet zone. Visits home gardens adjoining good-quality forest, but not found in areas where virgin forest is absent. **DISTRIBUTION** Lowlands to higher hills to about 1,300m. In higher hills, not as abundant as small Sri Lanka Dusky-striped Squirrel (p. 27), and absent at highest elevations. Confined to southern India and Sri Lanka. **BEHAVIOUR** Usually seen singly or in pairs. Nests in drey like Indian. Behaviour has many parallels with smaller Sri Lanka Dusky-striped. Both species often follow mixed species bird flocks in lowland rainforests such as Sinharaja and Morapitiya. Both are arboreal and come to the ground only where they have to cross a path to climb trees on the other side. Over the years has become tolerant of visitors at sites such as Sinharaja, where it come down to feeders. However, remains wary and takes flight at slightest hint of danger. **DIET** Mainly tender leaves, fruits, nuts, lichens and so on. Also insects, grubs and similar.

Prominent 'flame-stripe' on back

Indian Palm Squirrel ■ *Funambulus palmarum*

Most common squirrel, making its home in cities, home gardens and forests. Two pale stripes against dark back. **HABITAT** Although seen in urban environments, needs tall trees in which to roost at night or shelter during heat of day. **DISTRIBUTION** Four subspecies spread throughout the island to highlands. Species endemic to Indian subcontinent, found in southern India and Sri Lanka. **BEHAVIOUR** Has interesting symbiotic relationship with Yellow-billed Babblers,

and every flock of foraging babblers seems to have a pair of Palm Squirrels. Different pairs of squirrels holding territories in different parts will join flock of roving babblers. Unusually for a mammal, spends a good part of its time vocalizing. Repertoire limited to monotonously repeated, high-pitched call. Probably most vocal mammal in Sri Lanka. **DIET** Mainly plant matter like shoots, leaves, seeds and fruits. Occasionally insects and grubs.

Dry zone subspecies

Wet zone subspecies (subspecies not field diagnosable)

Sri Lanka Dusky-striped Squirrel ▪ *Funambulus obscurus*

Small dark squirrel. Can look darker than it is in dim recesses of rainforest. Three faint dorsal stripes on chocolate-brown coat. Tail not as long as body length, and relatively short tailed compared to other squirrels on the island. On first impressions, seems a bit misshapen because of short tail. Historically was considered endemic to southern India and Sri Lanka. Following a paper published by Rajith Dissanayaka and Tasuo Oshida, has become accepted as species endemic to Sri Lanka. **HABITAT** Where good-quality forest patches remain in wet zone. Tends to feed on lower to middle layer of trees, often going up and down trees. Scampers along fallen logs and explores crevices.

Indistinct stripes–looks all dark in poor light

DISTRIBUTION Wet zone from lowlands to highlands where good-quality forests remain. In Nuwara Eliya may be seen in Victoria Park, because Nuwara Eliya is surrounded by good-quality cloud forests in Mount Pedro Forest Reserve. **BEHAVIOUR** Occasionally runs across a footpath to gain access to trees on other side, but rarely feeds on the ground as the Indian Palm Squirrel (opposite) does at times. Mixed species feeding flocks in Sinharaja are almost always accompanied by one of these dainty squirrels. Often seen in pairs. Bird-like contact call. Will go about its business provided an observer stays still, but is a wary animal. **DIET** Mixed diet of flowers, tender shoots and fruits, as well as invertebrates such as insects and grubs. **WHERE TO SEE** Bird tables at Sinharaja. Also following mixed species feeding flocks. Easy to see in cloud forests in and around Horton Plains National Park.

Rare albino

Giant Grey Flying Squirrel ■ *Petaurista philippensis*

Spectacular to watch when engaging in long glide, but because of its nocturnal habits most people do not see it. Upperparts similar to black and yellow subspecies of the Grizzled Indian Squirrel (p. 30), but underparts pale not yellow. Overall appearance of large, blackish squirrel. Smaller Small Flying Squirrel *Petinomys fuscocapillus layardi* also pale on underparts, but rufous-chestnut on upperparts. Membranes on sides of body joined to fore and hind limbs, which are splayed out while gliding. **HABITAT** Appears most common in disturbed habitats, where tall trees are interspersed with open glades. Spends

the day and raises young inside tree hollow, so presence of old trees is probably limiting factor for providing daytime sleeping sites. **DISTRIBUTION** Mainly in mid-hills but ascending to highlands to Horton Plains. **BEHAVIOUR** Very little known about social organization. At sites such as the Hotel Tree of Life, a number of individuals seem to be concentrated in a small area. I have seen several feeding on a fruiting tree without any fighting taking place. **DIET** Bulk of diet seems to be fruits. Also eats tender shoots, bark and invertebrates. Visits home gardens to feed on mango and tamarind. **WHERE TO SEE** Hotel Tree of Life at Yahalathenna near Kandy has a colony that emerges at dusk (avoid using harsh spotlights in observations). Also seen at Jetwing Kaduruketha, near Wellawaya.

Long, bushy tail and 'wing' membranes

Small Flying Squirrel ■ *Petinomys fuscocapillus*

Gliding membranes less well developed than in Giant Grey Flying Squirrel (opposite). Underparts whitish with rufous tinge. Upperparts dark chestnut. Tail shorter than head and body length (HBL). **HABITAT** Tall forests. **DISTRIBUTION** Found in hills and ascends to highlands to 1,300m, and where central mountains slope down into north-central province and towards east in intermediate zone. Indian subcontinental endemic, confined to southern India and Sri Lanka. **BEHAVIOUR** Arboreal and nocturnal, spending day sleeping in tree hole. Very little known. **DIET** Probably variety of plant matter, including fruits and nuts. **WHERE TO SEE** At Kithulgala, on regular birding circuit, and Peak Wilderness, which is visited by local birders.

Dry zone subspecies brown

Wet zone subspecies black and yellow

Grizzled Indian Squirrel

■ *Ratufa macroura*

(Giant Squirrel)
Largest squirrel species in Sri Lanka.
Becomes habituated to people and readily
approaches them at picnic spots and hotels
to take fruits. **HABITAT** Requires forests
with tall, mature stands. **DISTRIBUTION**
Three subspecies spread throughout the
island, to highest mountains. **BEHAVIOUR**
Usually in pairs that maintain territory.
Loud, almost hysterical call, used to warn
of danger. **DIET** Wide range of plant
matter, from roots to leaves and fruits.
SUBSPECIES Highland subspecies *R. r.
macroura* similar to wet lowlands subspecies
by being black and yellow, but tail frosted
white. In wet lowlands subspecies *R. r.
melanochra* tail completely black. Subspecies
R. r. dandolena in dry lowlands distinctive,
being brown and buff. **WHERE TO SEE**
R. r. dandolena easily seen at camp sites in
national parks, *R. r. melanochra* in wet zone
rainforests like Sinharaja and *R. r. macroura*
in Horton Plains National Park.

CRICETIDAE (GERBILS)
This widespread rodent family is found in Asia, America and Europe. It includes the well-known lemmings and voles, and rats and mice of the New World. In Sri Lanka just one member is found in the subfamily Cricetinae, which also includes the hamsters that are kept as pets. Despite Sri Lanka having only one species, this is the second largest mammal family, with more than 600 species. Five subfamilies are recognized, including the subfamily Sigmodontinae, which contains the New World rats and mice.

Indian Gerbil ▪ *Tatera indica*

Besides the House Rat (p. 37), species most likely to be seen by visitors on a wildlife tour because of habit of foraging on forested tracks after nightfall. Looks quite pale in glare of headlights. Easily identified by long, fur-covered tail, with tuft of black fur at end – fully furred tail with pencil of hairs at end diagnostic. Bounding run different from scurrying run of House Rat; alternative common name, Antelope Rat, arises from this. **HABITAT** Range of habitats, from dry zone jungle to wet zone rainforest. Also plantations, which are a severely degraded habitat. However, does not seem able to compete with other rat and mouse species that are more common in urban environments with high human densities. **DISTRIBUTION** Throughout the island up to mid-hills.

Probably more common, if not more easily seen, in scrub-forested areas of dry lowlands. In areas such as Yala National Park I have noticed a very high density. **BEHAVIOUR** Gerbils are aggressive, and known to attack and kill animals larger than themselves. Both males and females dig their own burrows; females typically build two bolt holes. Does not habitually store food. Burrows often built on open ground without cover. Occasionally makes burrow within termite hill. Often seen when driving at night on forested roads in dry zone. **DIET** Omnivorous. Eats range of plant matter, from grain to seeds of introduced rubber tree. Also young birds, reptiles and even small mammals, as well as eggs, grubs, insects and similar.

Gerbils have tuft of black hair on tail-tip (not visible in picture)

> ### MURIDAE (RATS & MICE)
> This large family of rodents is the largest mammal family, with more than 700 species.
> They are indigenous to Europe, Asia and Australia, but humans have introduced them
> accidentally all over the world. Both murids (and cricetids) generally lack canines and
> premolars. Murids have long tails and in a few species the tail is prehensile (can be used
> as a fifth limb).

Lesser Bandicoot-Rat ▪ *Bandicota bengalensis*

Two species of bandicoot-rat in Sri Lanka can be separated from other Sri Lankan rodents
by their relatively large size, heavy build, and blunt and broad heads. Fur coarse and short
in both species. Tail relatively short and stout. Lesser is smaller of the two species. The
Greater Bandicoot-Rat (opposite) has larger hindfoot, over 50mm long, compared with
Lesser (under 40mm long). I have found Greater to be darker in colour but this is not a
reliable feature. **DISTRIBUTION** Throughout the island to highlands but most abundant
in wet zone and to elevations of 1,000m. **BEHAVIOUR** Nests in burrows and raises several
litters a year. Serious pest of paddy cultivation. **DIET** Mainly vegetarian; partial to rice
grain.

Note relatively short and stout tail

Greater Bandicoot-Rat ■ *Bandicota indica*

Largest of rat-like rodents, reaching HBL of 175mm. With tail, just under 30cm in length. Not aggressive, despite fierce appearance. Name bandicoot derives from Tamil word *pandicuttie* used in India to mean young pig, a reference to pig-like grunts uttered when it is frightened. Fur coarse and tail naked and scaly. Longish head with large ears. Young may be confused with Lesser Bandicoot-Rat (opposite). Besides overall size in adults, relatively large feet in relation to body and head size. **HABITAT** Found in human habitation, but does not habitually venture indoors as House Rats (p. 37) do. Particularly frequents areas near paddy fields, although every patch of scrub forest also holds bandicoots. **DISTRIBUTION** Throughout the island but seems less common in dry zone. Favours areas near water for building burrows, and a good swimmer. **BEHAVIOUR** Builds long galleries running along embankments of paddy fields. Side tunnels, employed to deposit earth away from main gallery, generally kept loosely plugged with earth, serving as emergency exits if a predator such as a Rat Snake enters burrow. Main gallery has at least one circular chamber used for raising young, as well as a few storage chambers where grain is stored. **DIET** Vegetarian, eating paddy and tuberous roots of plants such as yams and potatoes.

Coarse fur and large size

Indian Bush-Rat ■ *Golunda ellioti*

Short, rounded and furred ears, with tail length less than HBL. Tail hairy. More rounded muzzle and more rotund body relative to other rodents. Looks like a vole. Fur short and spiny. Not an urban rodent. **DISTRIBUTION** Wet zone in south-west, from lowlands to high elevations. Previous authors have considered populations below 1,000m elevation as different subspecies to highland populations. Endemic to Indian subcontinent, being confined to India and Sri Lanka. **BEHAVIOUR** During coffee-planting era, population explosions occurred. **DIET** Mainly vegetarian, but may eat invertebrates opportunistically. Constructs nests on the ground or in low bushes.

Vole-like shape

Eastern House Mouse ■ *Mus musculus*

Worldwide, house mice are found living with humans. In Sri Lanka, one of two mouse species that are small and without spiny fur on back. Similar Indian Field Mouse (opposite) told apart by white underparts, whereas Eastern has grey underparts. Naked tail about HBL or slightly longer. **DISTRIBUTION** Throughout the island in close association with humans. **BEHAVIOUR** Several litters produced annually. Nests anywhere that is dry and cosy, and where it can construct nest with straw, leaves or paper. **DIET** Omnivorous, eating wide range of plant and animal matter.

Grey underparts

Indian Field Mouse ▪ *Mus booduga*

Identified by small size, and fawn upperparts that contrast with white underparts. The Ceylon Field Mouse M. *cervicolor fulvidiventris* that W. W. A. Phillips refers to is what is now this species. The Fawn-coloured Mouse M. *cervicolor* does not occur in Sri Lanka. **HABITAT** Grassland, patanas and open areas. **DISTRIBUTION** Throughout the island. **BEHAVIOUR** Nocturnal and lives in short burrows with bolt holes at either end. **DIET** Grains, seeds and roots of grasses.

Fawn upperparts

White underparts

Sri Lanka Bi-coloured Spiny Mouse ▪ *Mus mayori*

Long head like rats in *Rattus* genus. Flattened spiny fur on back. Tail same length as HBL – a key field characteristic separating it from the Sri Lanka Spiny Mouse (p. 36). **HABITAT** Found foraging in grassland and near forested streams. **DISTRIBUTION** Highland subspecies with dull greyish-brown underparts typically occurs at more than 1,800m, with range extending on to Horton Plains. Subspecies in hills at around 1,000m has pure white underparts. Subspecies intergrade at lower levels where they meet. **BEHAVIOUR** Active by day and night. **DIET** Likely omnivorous, eating insects and small invertebrates as well as fruits.

Tail length equals HBL

Sri Lanka Spiny Mouse ■ *Mus fernandoni*

Similar to the Sri Lanka Bi-coloured Spiny Mouse (p. 35), with spiny fur on back mixed with shorter soft fur. Told apart by shorter tail and smaller feet. Tail noticeably shorter than HBL. Feet pure white. **DISTRIBUTION** Known mainly from dry lowlands in south-east. **BEHAVIOUR** Probably mainly nocturnal. Lives in burrows. **DIET** Probably plant matter. Little known about its ecology.

Tail length less than HBL

Montane Rat ■ *Rattus montanus*

The Montane Rat and Brown Rat (p. 38) both have a HBL of 18–27 cm. However, in terms of distribution, the highland subspecies of the House Rat (opposite) is the only species it is likely to be confused with. The latter is smaller with a HBL of 15–18 cm. Also, underparts of the Montane Rat are greyish-white and it is more stoutly built. The smaller Ohiya Rat (p. 39) is found in the same highland jungles but is easily separated by its bi-coloured tail. **DISTRIBUTION** Confined to highland cloud forests around Nuwara Eliya

including Horton Plains National Park. **BEHAVIOUR** W. W. A Phillips writes how this and other murids are found in a torpid state after gorging themselves on the seeds of *Strobilanthes*, which engage in periodic mass flowering. The species was found on one of these mass flowerings by Phillips, who first described it to science. **DIET** Feeds on the seeds and fruits of *Strobilanthes* spp. Diet may be broader to include invertebrates, but little is known about its ecology.

House Rat ■ *Rattus rattus*

(Black Rat)

Third largest of rat-like rodents in Sri Lanka. Larger rats (about 18–27cm HBL) found in Sri Lanka are Brown Rats (p. 38). House Rats smaller, with HBL of 15–18cm. Slim tail longer than HBL. **HABITAT** Thrives in and around human habitation because of ready supply of food from household waste. Fleas carried on body a vector for many diseases. **DISTRIBUTION** Throughout the island. **BEHAVIOUR** Similar to that of Brown Rat, which has been studied well. Rats seen scrambling up walls and along rafters are almost certainly House Rats. **DIET** Highly omnivorous, eating a variety of animal and vegetable matter, and even cakes of soap.

Less robust than bigger Brown Rat

Brown Rat ▪ *Rattus norvegicus*

Second largest of rat-like rodents in Sri Lanka. About 18–27cm HBL. House Rats (p. 37), with similar island-wide distribution, are smaller. Tail stout at base and tail length less than HBL. Blunt muzzle, finely furred short ears, large feet and scaly tail. Stout, heavy build and shaggy fur help separate it from the House Rat. **HABITAT** Prefers areas near water. Thrives in and around human habitation because of ready supply of food from household waste. **DISTRIBUTION** Throughout the island. W. W. A. Phillips believed it to be confined mainly to larger port cities such as Colombo, Galle and Trincomalee. This may still be the case. Believed to have originated in north Asia and subsequently spread worldwide through human activity. Brown Rats in Sri Lanka probably arrived on trading ships. **BEHAVIOUR** Peculiar mating system, in which several males mate with one female without any apparent competition between them. However, a male that is mating will subsequently mate more times with a female, possibly a strategy to improve its chances of being the one to inseminate the female. Females build nest in hole lined with straw, dead leaves, paper and so on. Young of rats and mice may use ultrasonic squeaks to communicate with the mother. Rats may only live to two years of age, but females are sexually mature by six months and may raise as many as 4–5 broods each year. Most likely to be encountered near ground level. Smaller, darker rats seen scrambling up walls and along rafters are more likely to be House Rats. **DIET** Highly omnivorous, eating a variety of animal and vegetable matter.

Heavy build

Ohiya Rat (Sri Lanka Bi-coloured Rat) ■ *Srilankamys ohiensis*

The name refers to this species being described from Ohiya in the highlands near Horton Plains. Readily identified by its bi-coloured tail; dark on upperside and pale on underside. Tail-tip completely pale. Fur on upperparts steely grey. Head proportionally large with conspicuous ears. Feet covered in white fur. Underparts white. **DISTRIBUTION** Most common in highlands, but has also been recorded in lowland rainforests including Sinharaja and Kanneliya. **BEHAVIOUR** Nocturnal, not afraid of people. W. W. A. Phillips describes captive animals becoming quite tame. **DIET** Largely frugivorous.

Steely grey upperparts and disproportionally large head

Soft-furred Field Rat ■ *Millardia meltada*

Members of the genus *Millardia* are similar those in the genus *Rattus*. A key distinction when handled is suppression of the posterior sole pads, and soft fur. This species also has whitish underparts that help to separate it from rats. **DISTRIBUTION** Widespread in dry lowlands. **BEHAVIOUR** Lives in small clans of 5–6, burrowing into soil adjoining cultivated fields. **DIET** Feeds on succulent stems of young grasses, and grains and seed.

Soft fur distinguishes species from Rattus *rats*

Sri Lanka Highland Climbing Mouse ■ *Vandeleuria noltheni*

See next species for subtle differences in appearance. **DISTRIBUTION** In the highlands, as high as 2,000m but can descend to 1,300m. The elevational distribution may have some overlap with the Asiatic Long-tailed Climbing Mouse (p. 42). **BEHAVIOUR** Will sleep in nests of dead leaves or in birds' nests. Arboreal lifestyle. **DIET** Buds, flowers, seeds and fruits.

Dark rufescent-brown underparts

Asiatic Long-tailed Climbing Mouse
■ *Vandeleuria oleracea*

There are two similar climbing mice species in Sri Lanka, previously considered subspecies of each other. Both have small, compact bodies, very long tails, and cinnamon-fawn body with white underparts. This species is separated from the Sri Lanka Highland Climbing Mouse (p. 41) by having brighter cinnamon versus dark rufescent-brown upperparts. Also slightly smaller, with HBL of 75–88mm versus 83–87mm in the Sri Lanka Highland Climbing Mouse. **DISTRIBUTION** Widespread in lowlands ascending to about 1,300m. **BEHAVIOUR** Arboreal mouse that uses prehensile tail to move fast among branches. Can take over nests of birds as sleeping site. **DIET** Buds, flowers, seeds and fruits.

Cinnamon-fawn body and white underparts

> ## HYSTRICIDAE (PORCUPINES)
> Old World porcupines in the family Hystricidae are found in southern Europe, Africa and Asia. They all have spiny quills on the body and are mainly nocturnal. Sri Lanka has just one species. The porcupines of the New World are in a different family, the Erethizontidae, found in northern South America and North America. They are less strictly nocturnal and can climb trees, unlike Old World porcupines. The two families are not closely related although the porcupines are all rodents.

Indian Crested Porcupine ▪ *Hystrix indica*

Relatively common, but seldom seen because of strictly nocturnal behaviour. Usual clue to its presence is a discarded quill. Blackish-brown and white, clothed with quills, those on tail forming train. On entering an animal's flesh, quills are likely to work their way in because of their texture. In India, many tigers turned man-eaters after encounters with porcupines left them injured. In Sri Lanka, leopards probably leave porcupines alone as they have a good supply of alternative prey. **HABITAT** Prefers wooded habitats but has readily adapted to home gardens. Powerful digger and excavates its own sleeping burrows, so availability of sleeping sites does not become a limiting factor, and ability to feed on broad

Clothed with quills

Continued on p. 44.

Quills on back form a 'train'

Detail of tail

diet may explain its continued survival in urban habitats. **DISTRIBUTION** Throughout lowlands to highlands, but less common at higher elevations. **BEHAVIOUR** Usually seen in pairs. Sometimes several individuals may sleep together. Very resilient to human presence. **DIET** Wide range of plant matter, from roots and tender leaves to fruits. Feeds on fallen fruits from trees such as Jak *Artocarpus heterophyllus*, 'Goraka' *Garcinia quaesita* and Cashewnut *Anarcardium occidentale*, popular in home gardens. Also raids yams of plants such as introduced Manioc *Manihot esculenta*, planted in home gardens. **WHERE TO SEE** Night drives outside parks and suburban areas. It is likely that as Colombo continues to expand, porcupines, which are fair-sized mammals, will be lost from its suburbs unless large urban nature reserves are created to provide refuges for animals such as these.

> **LEPORIDAE (HARES & RABBITS)**
> Hares and rabbits are in the order Lagomorpha, which is distinguished from the order Rodentia by having two pairs of upper incisors. The second incisor is immediately behind the first and lacks a cutting edge. Both teeth are covered in enamel and are white, whereas in rodents they are generally orange. Lagomorphs comprise two families, the pikas (family Ochotonidae), absent in Sri Lanka, and the hares and rabbits (family Leporidae). The latter contains 11 genera, of which *Lepus* and *Sylvilagus* (an American family) contain 32 and 17 species respectively.

Black-naped Hare ■ *Lepus nigricollis*

(Indian Hare)

The only wild hare or rabbit species in Sri Lanka. Outside protected areas, nocturnal due to risk of poaching and threats from domestic dogs and cats. **HABITAT** Prefers forested areas interspersed with glades of grassland. Best seen in national parks such as Yala. **DISTRIBUTION** Throughout the island to highest mountains. **BEHAVIOUR** By day prefers to lie up in a 'form', a patch of vegetation into which it snuggles and and in which it is well camouflaged. Where protected, as in national parks, may be seen active by day, or at least in early mornings. Otherwise seen when emerging to roadside verges after dark. **DIET** Herbivorous. Grasses, shoots, young leaves and so on.

Distinctive long ears

SORICIDAE (SHREWS)

Shrews look similar to mice but in fact they are in a different order, the Soricomorpha (which includes insect-eating mammals such as shrews and moles), in the family Soricidae. Some members of the order are not strictly insectivorous and eat a variety of other invertebrates, including worms, slugs, crustaceans and arthropods.

Shrews have a mouse-like appearance with a number of special characteristics. They have long, mobile snouts with sensitive hairs (vibrissae) that help them hunt for prey. They have long tails, often exceeding the HBL. Unlike mice, they have small eyes. They have a very high metabolic rate and many have to eat their own body weight every night. Researchers who use small mammal traps need to check regularly to ensure that any trapped shrews are released, otherwise they may starve to death. Shrews are also the smallest mammals in the world, with the Pygmy Shrew being the smallest.

Seven of the 10 shrews found in Sri Lanka are endemic. The work by Suyama Meegaskumbura and others using molecular techniques has shed light on their evolutionary relationships with the region's other shrews.

Horsfield's Shrew ▪ *Crocidura horsfieldii*

Greyish brown fur. Tail shorter than HBL. Feet have small claws. Separated from the Pygmy Shrew (p. 52) by larger size and larger feet. Longer fur lacks glossy sheen. **DISTRIBUTION** Common in highlands at 1,000–2,000m. **BEHAVIOUR** Most active at night. Breeds in small burrows. Females give birth to 2–3 young. **DIET** Worms, insects and other invertebrates of leaf litter.

Greyish-brown fur lacking glossy sheen

Sri Lanka Long-tailed Shrew ■ *Crocidura miya*

The two shrews in the genus *Crocidura* compared to the other shrews found in Sri Lanka are more mouse-like and have longer greyish-brown fur. Separated from Horsfield's Shrew (opposite) by tail longer than HBL; the only shrew in Sri Lanka to have this feature. Horsfield's is smaller with HBL 63.5mm versus 88.9mm in Sri Lanka Long-tailed. **DISTRIBUTION** Found from 900m to 2,000m in highlands. **BEHAVIOUR** Very little known. **DIET** Very little known.

Tail length more than HBL

Sinharaja Shrew ■ *Crocidura hikmiya*

Distinguished from other shrews mainly by examining skeletal features especially of head, together with mitochondrial DNA analysis. Shorter tail than in the Sri Lanka Long-tailed Shrew (p. 47). In a paper published by Suyama Meegaskumbura and others, the authors concluded that the two are sister species. Sinharaja confined to mid-montane and lowland rainforests in south-western Sri Lanka, Sri Lanka Long-tailed to montane forests of central hills (>900m); Horsfield's Shrew (p. 46) found from lowlands to mid-elevations. Sinharaja medium sized with HBL 75–83mm and tail length 90–100mm; Horsfield's smaller, with HBL 62–68mm and tail 49–55mm; Sri Lanka Long-tailed HBL 64.9–73.4mm and tail 92.8–100.3mm. With measurements taken with due note of elevation, it should be possible

to distinguish the three species. There is no easy way to tell them apart otherwise, although Long-tailed's tail being nearly 50 per cent of HBL is a strong clue to its identity, together with high, forested elevations. Sinharaja described as being dark grey-brown on upperparts and paler on underside, versus Sri Lanka Long-tailed being brown on upperparts and only slightly lighter coloured on underparts. **DISTRIBUTION** Only known from Sinharaja Rainforest both in lower elevations at Kudawa and higher eastern elevation at Morningside. **BEHAVIOUR** Very little known. **DIET** Probably similar to that of other shrews, comprising worms, grubs, insects and other invertebrates.

Dark grey-brown upperparts

Kelaart's Long-clawed Shrew ■ *Feroculus feroculus*

This and Pearson's Long-clawed Shrew (p. 50) occupy a similar range and need to be separated from each other. Both have forefeet with large claws. The key diagnostic feature is Kelaart's moderately long tail. In Pearson's tail is around half the HBL. Also, Kelaart's has long outstanding hairs on its tail, scattered throughout its length. Both species have small ears that are fully furred. **DISTRIBUTION** In central highlands ascending to Horton Plains. Found in damp habitats close to streams. Such a marked preference to wet habitats that Dr Kelaart, who discovered it, thought it may be a water shrew. **BEHAVIOUR** Very little known. **DIET** Probably a wide range of small invertebrates as well as plant matter.

Forefeet with strong claws; moderately long tail

Pearson's Long-clawed Shrew ■ *Solisorex pearsoni*

Large forefeet with long claws, hindfeet small. Separated from similar Kelaart's Long-clawed Shrew (p. 49) by smooth tail lacking long outstanding hairs scattered along length of Kelaart's. Another key field identification characteristic is shorter tail, about half the HBL. Both species have small ears, which are fully furred. Keelart's has 18 teeth in upper jaw; Pearson's has 16. **DISTRIBUTION** Recorded from Matale hills to highlands, at elevational range of 1,200–2,300m. Elevational range overlaps with Kelaart's. Also shares similar preference for damp habitats. **BEHAVIOUR** Very little known. **DIET** May be an obligate carnivore.

Forefeet with strong claws; smooth tail

House Shrew ▪ *Suncus murinus*

(Common Musk Shrew)

Most common of the shrews, found in houses even in large cities such as Colombo. Largest of 10 shrew species in Sri Lanka. Depending on subspecies, colour varies from bluish-grey to blackish-brown. One pair made a nest in the map cabinet in my house in Colombo, having carefully shredded several maps to create the equivalent of dry leaves. Like all shrews, has long, pointed, mobile snout with a number of long hairs (vibrissae) that are very sensitive to touch and enable it to detect prey in the dark. Utters high-pitched squeaks that give its presence away. **DISTRIBUTION** Throughout the island. **BEHAVIOUR** Nocturnal animal, although emerges at times at dusk. Aggressive towards its own species and others. Most shrew species eat their own body weight in the course of a night, because of a high metabolic rate. Very little is known of behavioural aspects of Sri Lankan shrews, but clearly olfactory communication (scent-marking) plays an important part. This species also known as the Musk Shrew due to musky odour it leaves behind from scent glands on its flanks. I can often smell when a Musk Shrew has left its calling card in my kitchen in search of geckos and spiders. **DIET** Readily eats geckos and small lizards in a house. Much of prey is invertebrates such as worms, insects and spiders, but when food is scarce will also eat vegetable matter such as fruits and grains.

Largest shrew, found in urban environments

Pygmy Shrew ■ *Suncus etruscus*

Smallest of Sri Lankan mammals, with HBL under 5cm. Tail shorter than HBL. Identified by small size, tiny feet and glossy fur. Molecular work by Suyama Meegaskumbura confirms that it is distinct from the Sri Lanka Pygmy Shrew (opposite), a sister species. Latter previously treated as subspecies of Pygmy, which has a wide distribution, from Europe and Africa to Asia. **DISTRIBUTION** Mainly in hills from 1,000m to high elevations of 2,000m. Also lowlands. **BEHAVIOUR** Active day and night. Hunts in leaf litter. **DIET** Worms, grubs, insects and other invertebrates.

Smallest Sri Lankan mammal

Sri Lanka Pygmy Shrew ■ *Suncus fellowesgordoni*

Very small, and at one time considered subspecies of the Pygmy Shrew (opposite). Short, velvety fur. Prominent naked ears. Small, neat feet with tiny claws. HBL 46–58mm. Tail 31–37mm. Larger than Pygmy and darker. In the hand, distinguished by two denticulations on lower incisors, absent in Pygmy. **HABITAT** Understorey of hill forests. **DISTRIBUTION** Confined to elevations at about 1,100–2,000m. Molecular phylogenetics suggest it is a sister species to the Malayan Pygmy Shrew *S. malayanus*, from Southeast Asia, possibly a relict species descended from a species once widespread across south Asia to Southeast Asia. **BEHAVIOUR** Little known. **DIET** Probably similar to that of other shrews.

Dark, velvety fur

Highland Shrew ■ *Suncus montanus*

Dark shrew once considered to be same species as the Hill Shrew S. *niger* in India, until split in 2008 by Suyama Meegaskumbura and Christopher J. Schneider. Small and dark. W. W. A. Phillips considered it a subspecies of the House Shrew (p. 51). HBL 91–115mm. Tail 65–72mm. Tail tapers gradually. **HABITAT & DISTRIBUTION** Forests from 1,000m to highest peaks. **BEHAVIOUR** When feeding, like other shrews presses down on food with forefeet and tears it with incisors. Shrews do not sit up like rodents. **DIET** Wide range of prey, from insects, worms and other invertebrates, to eggs of birds and lizards, and fruits and seeds. W. W. A. Phillips noted that shrews caught in traps are sometimes half eaten by other shrews.

Dark colouration

BATS

Bats (order Chiroptera) represent a fifth of all mammal species and have achieved true flight in the same fashion as birds and flying insects. Traditionally, they were split into two suborders, the Megachiroptera or megabats (fruit bats) and the Microchiropetra or microbats (insectivorous bats). Molecular phylogenetics have blurred this distinction and the current thinking is that megabats are nested within four large microbat lineages. Bats are believed to have evolved in the early Eocene Epoch, 50–52 million years ago. Three of the four main bat lineages arose in Laurasia, with one having arisen in Gondwana. The Laurasian lineages may have evolved in North America. Modern molecular phylogenies suggest two suborders, the Yinpterochiroptera, comprising the superfamilies Rhinolophoidea (leaf-nosed and horseshoe bats, and false vampires), and Pteropodidae (fruit bats); and the Yangochiroptera suborder with three superfamilies (Emballonuroidea, Noctilionoidea and Vespertilionoidea).

Anyone with a serious interest in the bats of Sri Lanka should refer to *Manual of the Mammals of Sri Lanka* and *A Field Guide to the Bats of Sri Lanka* (p. 171). Work led and supervised by Professor Wipula Yapa has resulted in a steady and significant number of scientific papers on bats. Yapa has for many years managed and supervised local postgraduate students, collaborating with overseas scientists to train local students and field staff and to ensure field studies use the latest in field techniques, hardware and software.

The well-known vampire bats in the Phyllostomidae family are restricted to South and Central America. Most microchiropterans feed on insects taken on the wing or picked off the ground. However, false vampire bats (family Megadermatidae) take larger, vertebrate prey such as geckos and skinks. Bats have their own distinctive flight patterns and characteristic heights at which they fly. One of the best ways to identify them is by using a bat detector, which converts their high-frequency calls outside the range of human hearing into a range which people can hear.

Pteropodidae (Fruit Bats)

This Old World family contains the largest bat species. Fruit bats have large eyes and vision is important to them for navigation and finding food. Fruit is the main component of their diet. Most of the 170 species in this family do not use echolocation, except for bats in the genus *Rousettus*.

Lesser Short-nosed Fruit Bat ■ *Cynopterus brachyotis*

One of four species of fruit bat on the island. This species and Leschenault's Rousette (p. 60), with body length of about 100mm, less than half the length of a flying fox. Colour

of fur on back and nape in this species has reddish tinge but can vary with age and sex. Fur on neck can be quite reddish in some individuals. See comments on measurements under Greater Short-nosed Fruit Bat (opposite). Generally Lesser is smaller in all respects. **HABITAT** Can tolerate disturbed habitats and also found in forests. **BEHAVIOUR** Roosts inside seed clusters of *kithul* trees, biting off seed strings to excavate roosting cavity. **DISTRIBUTION** Elevations above 1,000m. Previously thought to be smaller highland subspecies of Greater. **DIET** Mainly fruits, and also flowers.

Fur on neck quite reddish in some individuals

Greater Short-nosed Fruit Bat ■ *Cynopterus sphinx*

Forearm and ear longer than in the Lesser Short-nosed Fruit Bat (opposite). Species look similar and hard to tell apart. Pale fingers contrast with dark brown membranes. Juveniles olive. Breeding adults develop orange fur on throat and back. Forearm measurements of Greater 64–72mm, Lesser 56–64mm. Lesser also has small ears, under 18mm. Species hard to tell apart without measurements and at one time were considered to be subspecies. Fingers (phalanges) brownish-white. Prominent, white ear border. **HABITAT** Frequent visitor to home gardens even in largest cities. Needs palm trees on which to roost. **DISTRIBUTION** Up to mid-hills at around 800m. Most common in dry zone. As a rule of thumb, bat of lower elevations of the two near-identical species. **BEHAVIOUR** Roosts

Continued on p. 58.

Measurements usually required to separate species from the Lesser Short-nosed Fruit Bat

communally in small groups. A few individuals will roost together on same palm frond. Like the Indian Flying Fox (opposite), orientates entirely by vision. May also have keen sense of smell. In dry lowlands, especially in north, roosts hanging from leaves of the Talipot Palm *Corypha umbraculifera*. In wet zone creates roosting hollow among seed clusters of the Fishtail Palm, or *kithul* tree, *Caryota urens*. **DIET** Very fond of fruits of mango tree *Mangifera indica*, Banana *Musa* spp., Soursop *Annona muricata* and Guava *Psidium guajava*, all introduced plants found in home gardens. Also feeds on flowers.

Indian Flying Fox ▪ *Pteropus medius*

Unmistakable, with 122cm wingspan. Easily the largest bat found in Sri Lanka. Face very dog- or fox-like. Fur on face has yellowish tinge contrasting with dark wings. Roosts on tall trees and often found on roosts beside busy roads. **HABITAT** I cannot recall coming across a colony in a wooded area remote from human habitation. This may be because foraging in home gardens and plantations provides a much higher nutritional yield and foraging efficiency for the animals than foraging in native forests. **DISTRIBUTION** Up to mid-hills to around Kandy, although ascends as high as 2,000m. A few colonies found higher up. Absent from very highest elevations, but during fruiting may seasonally visit higher elevations. **BEHAVIOUR** Roosts communally in single tall tree or cluster of tall trees. Given away by noise it makes – there seems to be much bickering and quarrelling going on in a colony. From time to time a few bats fly around a roost by day, but they never feed until after dark, when they peel off one by one. Forages individually, occasionally uttering contact call in flight. After landing on tree, can move quite fast on branch by using 'hand-over-hand' motion. **DIET** Feeds exclusively on fruits and considered a pest of fruit plantations. Frequent visitor to home gardens to feed on jak, mango and pawpaw.

Face very dog-or fox-like

Leschenault's Rousette ■ *Rousettus leschenaultii*

Can be separated from similar short-nosed fruit bats by longer muzzle and absence of white lining on phalanges. **HABITAT** Preferentially a cave dweller, but also uses sites such as abandoned buildings and tunnels. **DISTRIBUTION** Widespread from lowlands to higher hills. May be absent in arid north. **BEHAVIOUR** Unlike other fruit bats, roosts communally in caves. Also unlike other fruit bats, can use echolocation to navigate in the dark when inside a cave. Uses excellent eyesight to locate food. Chamara Amerasinghe, who studied bats for his PhD, told me that this was the 'most innocent and complacent bat when captured' (note that no one who has not been trained should attempt to handle bats, and those undertaking research should be inoculated for rabies). **DIET** Wide range of fruits and flowers.

Long muzzle

Uses excellent eyesight to locate food

> ## MEGADERMATIDAE (FALSE VAMPIRE BATS)
> Found in the Old World tropics and subtropics, these are large bats with ears that
> are joined up near the bases. The tragus is long and divided into two parts of unequal
> length. Each part is pointed, forming a two-pronged tragus. The prominent noseleaf
> and long ears make the bats easy to identify. They have short, broad wings that give
> them good manoeuvrability. They are not related to the blood-drinking vampire bats
> found in South America. They are carnivorous, eating a broad range of other small
> vertebrates, including reptiles, amphibians and mammals.

Greater False Vampire ▪ *Megaderma lyra*

Forearm length 67–70mm compared to 50–59mm in the Lesser False Vampire (p. 62).
Other differences allow the two species to be easily told apart. See description of Lesser
for details. **DISTRIBUTION** More common in wet lowlands than in dry zone. Ascends
to mid-hills to about 1,000m. **BEHAVIOUR** Roosts in small colonies in caves, tunnels
and abandoned houses. Enters houses to pluck geckoes off walls. Hunts low with slow,
flapping flight. **DIET** Preys on large insects and small vertebrates, including small reptiles,
amphibians, birds and even small mammals.

Ear join higher than in the Lesser False Vampire   *Top of noseleaf flat, with straight sides*

Lesser False Vampire ▪ *Megaderma spasma*

This and the Greater False Vampire (p. 61) lack tail. In both species ears joined above head. In Lesser join is lower down and ears are proportionately slimmer. Lesser smaller but size may not be apparent in the field. Noseleafs differ: in Lesser, posterior noseleaf

(upper leaf) rounded at top and sides and curved inwards; in Greater, top of noseleaf flat and sides straight. In Lesser, intermediate noseleaf heart shaped and broad. In Greater it is narrow. Both species have greyish, silky

fur. **DISTRIBUTION** Widespread (but uncommon) in lowlands and ascending up to higher hills. May be absent in highlands. **BEHAVIOUR** Roosts in caves, tree hollows and houses. **DIET** Low flying; gleans insects from trees. Occasionally takes small vertebrates such as amphibians.

Long, slim ears

Intermediate noseleaf heart shaped and broad

Ears join lower than in the Greater False Vampire; also proportionatelly slimmer

> **RHINOLOPHIDAE (HORSESHOE BATS)**
> This family contains one genus, *Rhinolophus*, which is found across Europe, northern Africa and Asia. The bats get their name from the anterior (lower) noseleaf, which is horseshoe shaped and curves around the nostrils. The intermediate noseleaf has a raised fleshy projection called the sella. The posterior (upper) noseleaf has an upwards-pointing, fleshy protuberance called the lancet. The shape of the sella and how it is connected to the rest of the noseleaf varies with species, and is useful for identifying different species. A tragus is absent in this family. The bottoms of the ears have a prominent fold called the antitragus. This looks superficially like a second ear structure, whereas in *Hipposideridae* species the antitragus looks more like an upwards fold of the bottom of the earlobe. The bats' echolocation abilities allow them to fly low over the ground and navigate through trees and bushes while hunting for insects.

Lesser Woolly Horseshoe Bat ■ *Rhinolophus beddomei*

Larger of two *Rhinolophus* species found in Sri Lanka, with forearm of 54–59mm. Intermediate leafnose (sella) trifoliate. In the Rufous Horseshoe Bat (p. 64) it is simple. Ears large and pointed. Woolly fur grizzled grey-brown.
DISTRIBUTION Recorded throughout the island to highlands, but more common from lowlands to higher hills. Confined to India and Sri Lanka, and the one in Sri Lanka is a potential split. **BEHAVIOUR** Roosts communally in caves, tunnels and abandoned buildings. **DIET** Insectivorous. Feeds on moths, beetles, termites, mosquitoes and similar.

Ears large and pointed

Fur grizzled grey-brown

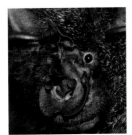

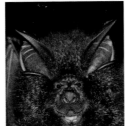

Intermediate leafnose trifoliate

Rufous Horseshoe Bat ■ *Rhinolophus rouxii*

Smaller of two *Rhinolophus* species found in Sri Lanka, with forearm of 47–54mm. Intermediate leafnose simple. See Lesser Woolly Horseshoe Bat (p. 63) for comparison. Colour on back variable, from brown to reddish-brown. There may be a seasonal change in colour. Usual colour reddish-brown. Easily separated from Lesser Woolly by reddish colour and simple noseleaf. **HABITAT & DISTRIBUTION** In and near forests in wet and

Colour variable from brown to rufous

Intermediate leafnose simple

dry zones. Population has crashed during the last century and it is no longer one of the most common bats. **BEHAVIOUR** Roosts communally in caves, tunnels and abandoned buildings. Often found in mixed species roosts. Low-flying, and may enter buildings in pursuit of insects. **DIET** Insectivorous. Feeds on moths, beetles, termites, mosquitoes and similar.

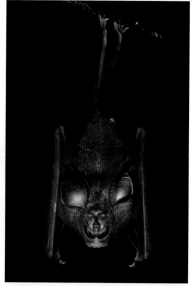

Intermediate leafnose simple

Hipposideridae (Leaf-nosed or Round-leaf Bats)

This is an Old World family of the tropics and subtropics. The genus *Hipposideros* contains about 80 species. The family is similar to the Rhinolophidae in having a complex noseleaf. The anterior noseleaf (the lower) is rounded and forms a weak horseshoe shape. The intermediate noseleaf is loosely rectangular and lacks the fleshy projection (sella) found in horseshoe bats. The posterior (upper) noseleaf is rounded on top, and is divided into vertical pockets with structures known as septa. The lower noseleaf is typically supplemented by additional lateral leaflets, the number of of which varies with species – it is sometimes necessary to count them to tell the species apart. The well-developed tail is contained within the interfemoral membrane. The pointed ears have conspicuous serrations or ridges on the inner lobes.

Dusky Leaf-nosed Bat ■ *Hipposideros ater*

Small, with forearm about 35–37mm. No supplementary leaflets. Large ears rounded and lack pointiness of other *Hipposideros* species. Well-developed antitragus. Ears have fur at

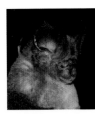

bases. Hairs on back silky white, terminating in colour varying from black to bright chestnut. When fur is ruffled it has a two-tone colour, giving rise to other common name of Bi-coloured Leaf-nosed Bat. **DISTRIBUTION** Mainly lowlands; absent from hills. Most common in wet zone lowlands. **BEHAVIOUR** Roosts communally in caves and tunnels. Unless it is in a very deep sleep, ears twitch constantly. Undertakes considerable grooming by day. Low, fluttering flight. **DIET** Insectivorous. Feeds on small beetles and low-flying insects.

No supplementary leaflets; rounded ears

Fulvous Leaf-nosed Bat
■ *Hipposideros fulvus*

Small, with forearm about 40mm. No supplementary leaflets as in the Dusky Leaf-nosed Bat (opposite). Large ears broad based and rounded at tips; more clearly rounded than in Dusky. Fur varies from grey to orange. Bases of hairs lighter in colour. On the wing, fourth metacarpal is seen to be longer than fifth. **DISTRIBUTION** Throughout lowlands. **BEHAVIOUR** Roosts in caves, tunnels and abandoned buildings. Sometimes with other bat species. Hunts in small groups. **DIET** Insectivorous. Feeds on beetles and moths.

No supplementary leaflets; broad-based ears

Cantor's Leaf-nosed Bat ■ *Hipposideros galeritus*

Medium-sized, with forearm about 47–51mm. Two pairs supplementary leaflets. Intermediate noseleaf wider than posterior (upper). Larger noseleaf than in Schneider's Leaf-nosed Bat (p. 71), and noseleaf squarish. Anterior noseleaf (lower leaf) extends almost to end of muzzle. Posterior noseleaf divided into four cells. Large, broad ears with antitragus forming spine-like projection on base. Ears clothed with fur. Body fur silky and long. Back reddish-brown to black. **DISTRIBUTION** Lowlands to mid-hills. **BEHAVIOUR** Roosts in family parties. Uses caves and abandoned buildings. **DIET** Beetles, moths and other low-flying insects.

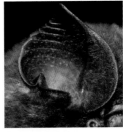

Two supplementary leaflets   *Antitragus 'spine'*

Intermediate noseleaf wider than posterior (upper)

Body fur silky and long

Great Leaf-nosed Bat ■ *Hipposideros lankadiva*

Large, with forearm about 78mm. Three supplementary leaflets on both sides next to noseleaf. Largest insectivorous bat in Sri Lanka. Short, dense fur brown and does not extend to membranes.

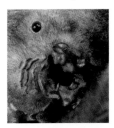 

DISTRIBUTION Lowlands and ascending higher hills. Most common in wet zone.

BEHAVIOUR Flies low, using echolocation to thread its way through trees and branches. Roosts communally in caves and tunnels.

DIET Beetles and other slow-flying insects.

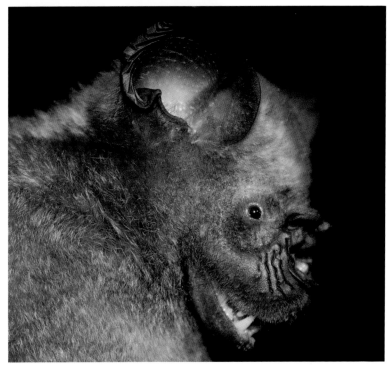

Three supplementary leaflets

Schneider's Leaf-nosed Bat

■ *Hipposideros speoris*

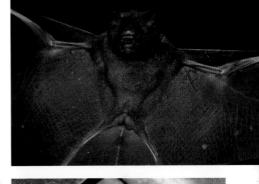

Medium-sized, with forearm about 50–54mm. Three supplementary leaflets. Noseleaf small. Posterior leaf broader than anterior and divided into four cells. Short, dense fur varies from reddish-brown to golden-brown. On the base of the ear, the antitragus forms

Continued on p. 72.

Antitragus 'spine'

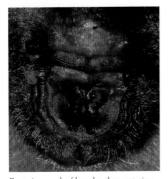

Posterior noseleaf broader than anterior

Fur reddish- to golden-brown

a conspicuous spine-like projection. **DISTRIBUTION** Widespread from lowlands to highlands. Confined to India and Sri Lanka. **BEHAVIOUR** Roosts in caves and tunnels. They have an odour. Hunts low-flying insects. Enters houses to pick off insects. **DIET** Insectivorous. Feeds on beetles and mosquitoes.

Three supplementary leaflets

Emballonuridae (Sac-winged & Sheath-tailed Bats)
This diverse family is found in the Old and New Worlds. Sac-winged bats have a pouch on the leading edge of the wing that is believed to disperse a scent used for communication. Sheath-tailed bats get their name from the tail being encased for a greater part of its length by a membrane between the legs (interfemoral membrane). Emballonurids have simple ears that are often joined by a band of skin across the forehead.

Pouch-bearing Bat

■ *Saccolaimus saccolaimus*

(Bare-rumped Sheathtail Bat)
Pronounced gular sac, but wing
pouches (radio metacarpal pouches)
seen in genus *Taphozous* are
absent. Male has bigger gular sac
than female. Conical muzzle with
forwards-facing nostrils and large
eyes. Lower lip has groove. Small ears

Conical muzzle and forwards-facing nostrils

with fluted margins.
Dark velvety-brown
on back with flecks
of white hair. Overall
impression is of long-
winged, dark bat with
pouch under chin.
DISTRIBUTION
Widespread in
lowlands ascending
to mid-hills, from
India to Southeast
Asia. **BEHAVIOUR**
Typically found
roosting communally
in tree hollows but may
also use abandoned
buildings. Flies at
height of 100m or so at
dusk for feeding, and
has habit of squealing.
DIET Insectivorous.
Feeds on beetles,
termites and similar.

Short tail emerging from interfemoral membrane

Long-winged Tomb Bat ■ *Taphozous longimanus*

Both the Long-winged and Black-bearded Tomb Bat (opposite) have a wing-pouch (radio metacarpal pouch). In Long-winged chin is naked. Male Black-bearded has black hairs on chin, and female has furry chin, although may lack black beard. Male Long-winged

has gular pouch that is absent in female; Black-bearded lacks gular pouch. Long-winged has short, dense fur extending to wing membranes. Colour varies from fulvous to cinnamon-brown. Conical muzzle with forwards-facing nostrils that have groove between them. **HABITAT & DISTRIBUTION** Lowlands, especially where palms are found. **BEHAVIOUR** Fast and high-flying. Roosts in crowns of palm trees, as well as tree hollows, rocky niches and old buildings. **DIET** Insectivorous. Feeds on beetles and moths.

Naked chin

Short, dense fur extending to wing membranes

Black-bearded Tomb Bat

■ *Taphozous melanopogon*

Three species of sheath-tailed bat occur in Sri Lanka

and this one is easily identified by presence of 'black beard' under chin in male. Unlike the Long-winged Tomb Bat (opposite), Black-bearded does not have gular pouch.

DISTRIBUTION Found in lowlands.
DIET Insectivorous.

Adult males have 'black beard' under chin

> **MOLOSSIDAE (FREE-TAILED BATS)**
> This family of Old and New World bats is characterized by tails that extend beyond the interfemoral membrane. The bats typically have a short muzzle with fleshy lips. The tragus is tiny with an antitragus that is well developed. The long, narrow wings are designed for flight in open spaces, and are required to help them launch themselves from a height to enable them to gain lift. Their feet and nose-pads have sensory bristles. Their ears are large and fleshy, with an ill-defined shape.

Wrinkle-lipped Free-tailed Bat ▪ *Chaerephon plicatus*

Similar to the Egyptian Free-tailed Bat (opposite), with both possessing fat lips that are wrinkled. Both species were once placed in the genus *Tadarida*. There are two key differences between the species. In Wrinkle-lipped, inner bases of ear margins are clearly

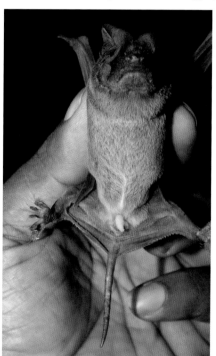

joined and form distinct band across forehead. Also, more than half of tail is free (not contained within interfemoral or 'tail membrane'). Premaxillae united; separate in Egyptian (premaxillae are bone structures to which incisor teeth are connected, a feature that museum taxonomists can examine). Fur also deeper chocolate colour than in Egyptian. Upper lip hangs over lower lip. **DISTRIBUTION** Recorded in the past in lower slopes of central highlands and in dry lowlands. **BEHAVIOUR** Fast and high flying. Roosts communally in caves and crevices. **DIET** Insectivorous.

More than half of tail is 'free'

Wrinkled, fat lips

Egyptian Free-tailed Bat
■ *Tadarida aegyptiaca*

Similar to the Wrinkle-lipped Free-tailed Bat (opposite), with both possessing fat lips that are wrinkled. In Egyptian, inner bases of ear margins not joined by band on forehead. Only up to half of tail is free. Premaxillae separate; joined in Wrinkle-lipped. Upper lip hangs over lower lip. **DISTRIBUTION** Mainly foothills of central highlands. **BEHAVIOUR** Mature females bigger and form maternity colonies. Fast-flying, little-known bat. **DIET** Insectivorous. Feeds on beetles, termites, moths and similar.

Calcar

Upper lip hangs over lower lip

> ## VESPERTILIONIDAE (EVENING & VESPER BATS)
> This very large family comprises nearly 500 species in about 50 genera. It is the second largest of the mammal families (the Muridae comprises more than 1,000 species). The family has four subfamilies, all of which are represented in Sri Lanka (Vespertilioninae, Myotinae, Murininae and Kerivoulinae). Vespertilionids have simple muzzles and no complex noseleafs. The ability of some species to hibernate in winter has allowed them to colonize high latitudes.

Hardwicke's Woolly Bat ▪ *Kerivoula hardwickii*

Easily identified by small size, and funnel-shaped ears with long, attenuate tragi. Unlike the Painted Bat (opposite), wings are uniform dark brown. Membranes thin and translucent. **DISTRIBUTION** Very rare, known mainly from hills at about 1,000m. **BEHAVIOUR** In Borneo, roosts in the Raffles' Pitcher-plant *Nepenthes rafflesiana*. Its guano is an important source of nutrition for this carnivorous plant, which seems to have co-evolved to provide snug roosts for these small bats. Very little known in Sri Lanka. In other parts of range across Asia, known to hunt in dense forests, roosting in tree hollows and leaves. **DIET** Insectivorous.

Funnel-shaped ears

Painted Bat ■ *Kerivoula picta*

Distinctive bat with black and orange wings. Unlikely to be mistaken for any other bat in Sri Lanka. Long, woolly fur on body scarlet. Ears have long, slender tragi. Males slightly brighter than females. **DISTRIBUTION** Throughout lowlands to hills to about 1,000m, although may be found at even higher elevations. **BEHAVIOUR** Roosts by day on dead, down-hanging fronds of banana trees, as well as on sugar cane and grasses. Not easy to find. **DIET** Insectivorous. Hunts for insects in groves of plantains, and in patches of bushes and short trees. Fluttering flight similar to a large moth's.

Slender tragi

Distinctive black and orange wings

Round-eared Tube-nosed Bat ■ *Murina cyclotis*

Tiny, hairy bat, about 5cm in length. Like other members of the genus, has tube-nosed nostrils at end of longish muzzle. Ears directed forwards, with prominent tragi. Hairs on back reddish-fawn with grey bases. Easily identified by small size, tubular nostrils and overall rusty hue. **DISTRIBUTION** Recorded in central hills at about 1,000m, as well as in dry lowlands. **BEHAVIOUR** Roosts communally in caves, crevices or folds of large dead leaves (for example of Cardamom), which are hanging down. Hunts low down, with twists and turns, within a couple of metres from the ground. **DIET** Insectivorous.

Prominent tragi

Tube-nosed nostrils

Overall rusty hue

Van Hasselt's Mouse-eared Bat
■ *Myotis hasseltii*

Identified by warm brown fur, small size, and dingy white or yellowish-white underparts. Wings dark brown. Long ears with long tragus. Calcar is very long. Long tail is contained within interfemoral membrane. **DISTRIBUTION** Mainly known from dry lowlands but colonies also found in mountains, for example in Knuckles Range. **BEHAVIOUR** Small colonies roost in tree hollows, bamboo clumps and abandoned buildings. A trawling Myotis, that scoops insects from the surface of waterbodies. **DIET** Insectivorous. Feeds on mosquitoes and similar.

Long ears with long tragi

Warm brown fur colour

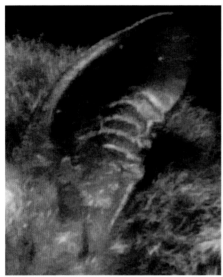

Long ears with long tragi

Horsfield's Mouse-eared Bat

▪ *Myotis horsfieldii*

Small, with dark brown to sooty-black fur. Long ears with long tragus. Forearm length averages 38mm. Long, rounded snout with pronounced glandular swelling between nostrils and eyes. Long, narrow ears. Long tail contained within interfemoral membrane. **HABITAT** Forests near waterbodies. **DISTRIBUTION** Recorded in wet zone hills and dry lowlands. May be more widely distributed than records suggest as was overlooked in the past. **BEHAVIOUR** Roosts in small to large colonies in caves, tunnels, tree hollows and similar. Hunts low over water. **DIET** Insectivorous. Feeds on mosquitoes and the like.

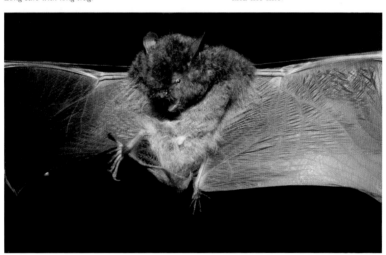

Long tail contained within interfemoral membrane

Kelaart's Pipistrelle ■ *Pipistrellus ceylonicus*

Face similar to those of other pipistrelles, with short, broad muzzle, with glandular swellings on either side. Back reddish-chestnut or brown with underparts paler. Wings brown. Eastern Bent-winged Bat (p. 89) has different head shape; wings not as long, narrow and pointed. Also, has much longer tail. **DISTRIBUTION** Widespread in wet zone ascending to highest elevations. May be the pipistrelle seen on a visit to Horton Plains. Seems more common in highlands. Distribution in dry lowlands patchy. **BEHAVIOUR** Roosts in small colonies in tree hollows, wells, crevices and abandoned buildings. Hunts low, constantly twisting and turning. **DIET** Insectivorous. Feeds on beetles and other flying insects.

Glandular swellings between nostril and eye

Indian Pipistrelle ■ *Pipistrellus coromandra*

This and the Pygmy Pipistrelle (p. 85) similar, being small, dark bats with glandular swellings between nostril and eye. Tragi end with rounded tip. Pygmy slightly smaller and usually darker. Safest way to tell them apart is by using measurements in the hand. It should also be possible to do so from their calls, using bat detectors. **DISTRIBUTION** Found throughout the island to about 1,300m. Most common in dry lowlands. **BEHAVIOUR** One of the earliest bats to emerge when there is still light in the sky. Often a group will forage together. Roosts in trees, old buildings or rocky crevices. **DIET** Insectivorous. Feeds on tiny insects including mosquitoes.

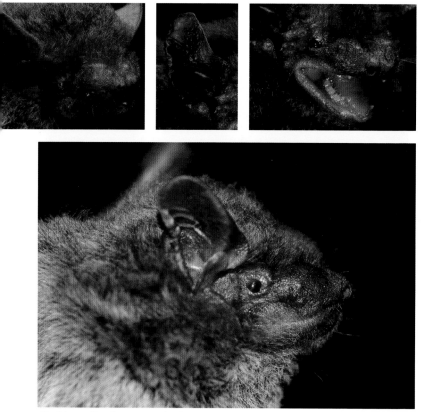

Glandular swellings between nostril and eye

Pygmy Pipistrelle ▪ *Pipistrellus tenuis*

Similar to the Indian Pipistrelle (p. 84), but generally darker and smaller. Difficult to separate in the field without taking measurements or studying vocalizations. Smallest bat found in Sri Lanka. Prominent calcars. Fur highly variable, but typically coffee-brown. **DISTRIBUTION** Mainly wet and intermediate zones ascending hills to 1,300m. Considered common in wet lowlands. Small bats that take to Colombo's skies at dusk are this species. **BEHAVIOUR** Roosts in trees, caves, buildings and roofs of houses. **DIET** Insectivorous. Feeds on tiny insects including mosquitoes.

Coffee-brown fur

Tickell's Bat ▪ *Hesperoptenus tickelli*

Broad, blunt muzzle, swollen on sides as in pipistrelles. Black eyes look small, between ears and glandular swellings. Ears yellowish-brown, with feet also having tiny golden hairs. Fur on back varies from greyish-yellow to bright golden-brown. Overall golden-brown hue of fur and reddish-brown on some of wing membranes make it easy to tell apart from similar species. One of the larger insectivorous bats, with forearm length of 61mm. **DISTRIBUTION** Recorded throughout lowlands ascending hills to 1,000m. More abundant in lowlands. **BEHAVIOUR** One of the earliest bats to come out at dusk. Flies over open spaces about 15m above the ground. **DIET** Insectivorous. Feeds on beetles, termites and similar.

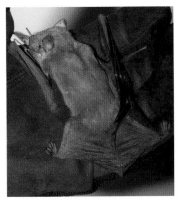

Fur greyish-yellow to golden-brown

Ears yellowish-brown

Broad, blunt muzzle swollen on sides

Asiatic Greater Yellow House Bat ▪ *Scotophilus heathii*

Bats in this genus, of which two are found in Sri Lanka, are medium sized, with short, rounded ears that are spaced well apart, and short, broad, swollen muzzle. Tragi crescent-shaped and rounded at tip. Colour of fur varies from yellowish-brown (hence the common name of Yellow Bat) to chestnut. Main difference between this and the Asiatic Lesser Yellow House Bat (see p. 88) is that latter has whitish underparts and shorter forearm. Adults of Greater always bigger, but young individuals may be same size as adult Lesser. One of the largest insectivorous bats. **DISTRIBUTION** Lowlands to hills to about 1,000m. Distribution in lowlands may be correlated to areas where coconut-palm plantations are found, such as in coastal belt. Once common in cities such as Colombo. **BEHAVIOUR** Roosts in palm trees, caves and buildings. **DIET** Insectivorous, foraging on large flying insects, beetles, moths and similar. Flies along straight line and retraces their path.

Short, rounded ears

Swollen muzzle; fur yellowish-brown to chestnut

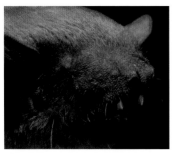

Short ears

Asiatic Lesser Yellow
House Bat ▪ *Scotophilus kuhlii*

Very similar to the Asiatic Greater Yellow
House Bat (see p. 87). Main difference is
that this species is smaller and has whitish
underparts. Short fur chestnut-brown with
yellowish hue in Asiatic. **DISTRIBUTION**
Dry lowlands in northern and eastern sectors.
BEHAVIOUR Roosts in palm trees, caves and
buildings. **DIET** Insectivorous, foraging on
flying insects.

Whitish underparts

> **MINIOPTERIDAE (LONG-FINGERED BATS)**
> Small-to medium-sized bats, with a simple muzzle and concealed tail. The second phalanx of the third finger is nearly three times the length of the first with a characteristically bent appearance, giving them the alternate name of Bent-winged bats. A single genus with 38 species worldwide.

Eastern Bent-winged Bat ■ *Miniopterous fuliginosus*

(Schreiber's Long-fingered Bat)

Small bat with short, very broad muzzle, a rounded/domed forehead and rhomboidal ears. Longest finger of wing extremely long and helps avoid confusion with Kelaart's Pipistrelle (p. 83). High forehead densely covered in fur. Short, triangular ears. Outer margins of ears form lobes near mouth. Overall dark bat, with blackish-brown fur. Second phalanx of third finger three times as long as first phalanx. **DISTRIBUTION** Mainly in mid-hills of wet zone at about 1,300m. May be absent from dry zone. **BEHAVIOUR** Roosts in large colonies in caves and rock crevices. **DIET** Insectivorous. Feeds on beetles, termites and similar.

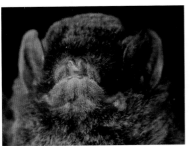
Overall dark colour

Short muzzle

Short, triangular ears

Outer ear margins form lobe near mouth

MANIDAE (PANGOLINS)
The order Pholidota contains only one family – the Manidae, with eight species in one genus, *Manis*. Four are found in Indomalaya, the other four in the tropical region of Africa. All share a triangular head with a pointed nose and body armour, and soft, exposed undersides. The ears are absent or nearly absent, and the lower jaw is toothless. Their very long tongue is extruded to capture ants and other insects. They are solitary, mainly nocturnal mammals that use scent marking to communicate.

Indian Pangolin ■ *Manis crassicaudata*

Unmistakable, with small, long head and scales on upper body. Scales provide defence against predators when it curls up to protect its soft underparts. Hard, sharp-edged scales can also inflict injuries. **HABITAT** Mix of forest habitats from dry thorn scrub to wet zone forests, where its main food, termites and ants, are found. Flesh considered tasty by some humans, and it has been eliminated from areas where it strays into contact with people.

The nocturnal pangolin is rarely seen during daytime

Scales provide defence against predators

DISTRIBUTION Up to mid-hills to about 1,300m. Distribution coincides with occurrence of its main prey, termites. **BEHAVIOUR** Appears naturally scarce as even in national parks, where it is protected, it is rarely seen at night. Outside protected areas, numbers may be very low due to it being hunted by people. Most of my records of it are from coming across the remains of a dead individual, although I once had the good fortune to watch a leopard cub of about 12 months playing with a pangolin. The pangolin feigned death, and the cub got bored and left it. Walks on sides of forefeet to reduce wear and tear on digging claws, which are strong enough to rip open anthills. Also climbs trees to devour ants from nests. **DIET** Feeds mainly on termites (white ants) and ants.

FELIDAE (CATS)

The Felidae comprises 37 cat species in 14 genera, naturally found around the world except in Australia and Antarctica. The family contains two subfamilies, the Pantherinae, which comprises seven big cat species, and the Felinae with 30 of the smaller cats. Of all carnivores, cats are the most specialized as meat eaters. Their short guts do not allow them to switch to vegetarian food sources.

Broadly speaking, cats employ two techniques for hunting: patrolling in search of prey or lying in wait. The background colour or ground colour of a cat's coat reflects the general colour of its habitat. In a forested environment where the trees create shadows and dappled light, the coat may be striped or spotted. The underneath of the tip of the tail can be white as in Cheetahs and leopards, to work as a visual cue. Cubs seem to find this useful in following their mother.

Cats have more developed senses than humans for sight, smell and hearing. For most cat species, vision is the most important of the senses. However, what is meant by better vision needs some clarification. Humans actually have a higher visual acuity, or ability to resolve detail under good light, than cats do. However, cats have more sensitive vision, especially under low light levels, and are about six times more sensitive to light than humans. As many cats are adept climbers, being able to judge distances accurately is important. Therefore, of the carnivores, the cats have the most developed binocular vision, but not as good as in humans.

Just as smell plays a small part in hunting, it is also a very important tool in communicating with other members of the same species. Cats scent mark their territories using a combination of methods. The most common is spraying urine. Another is using their faeces as markers. Yet another is 'scratching', where scent from inter-digital glands is mixed in.

Most cats lead a solitary existence. Lions are the only truly social cats, although bachelor groups of Cheetahs may hunt together.

A young leopard cub shows the white tips to the tail and the pale crescents on the back of the ears. Leopards of all ages have these and they may be used in visual communication.

Jungle Cat ■ *Felis chaus*

Elegant cat, reaching size of a small dog. When seen in the field, may look bigger than it really is – people imagine it to be as big as a jackal, but in fact it is smaller. Uniformly sandy-brown coat with greyish tone, and pointed ears. Underparts lighter. Tips of ears black. First impression on a daytime sighting is of a jackal-like animal. On close views, black barring on lower half of legs can be seen. Tail shows heavy black rings against silvery background. One of Sri Lanka's most beautiful mammals, though largely unknown and unnoticed because of its nocturnal habits. **HABITAT** Dry zone scrub forests are regular haunt. Regular sightings in Uda Walawe National Park demonstrate its preference for hunting in tall grassland. **DISTRIBUTION** Appears restricted to dry lowlands. I suspect the Jungle Cat is more abundant than suspected in dry zone areas, where prey such as the Indian Gerbil (Antelope Rat) is abundant. **BEHAVIOUR** Most sightings are of a single animal. May have usual felid social structure of male controlling home range that encompasses home range of several females.

Barred tail

Very little known about its behaviour in the wild. Can be seen hunting early in the morning and evening. Probably nocturnal, especially where there is a human presence. Despite the name, more of a grassland cat.

Continued on p. 94.

Pointed ears

Sandy-brown coat with greyish tones

DIET Predominantly small mammals such as hares, mouse-deer and rodents, and birds, eggs and so on. I once watched two Jungle Cats feasting on freshly hatched termites that

Tips of ears blackz

were emerging from the ground. **SUBSPECIES** Six subspecies recognized, distributed from Southeast Asia across south Asia to Middle East. Subspecies found in Sri Lanka, *F. c. kelaarti*, considered to be restricted to southern India and Sri Lanka. **WHERE TO SEE** Uda Walawe National Park on evening game drive the most reliable site. I have also come across it on public roads through dry zone forests, around midnight, when vehicular traffic is virtually absent. Serious cat enthusiasts could take a night drive on roads through or bordering grassland areas that adjoin national parks such as Yala. See night safaris (p. 168) and avoid using spotlights.

Elegant posture

Rusty-spotted Cat ■ *Prionailurus rubiginosa*

Smallest wild cat in Sri Lanka and rest of the world. Nearly the size of a small domestic cat, and may easily be overlooked for a feral cat. However, can be identified by white stripes on head, rusty spots on greyish-brown body and unmarked tail. Facial pattern similar to the Fishing Cat's (p. 96). **HABITAT** Needs forest cover. Found in tall forests in wet zone as well as in thorn scrub forests in dry zone. In both forest types, often encountered along forest trails. I have come across it hunting beside motorable dirt roads running though dry zone forests. **DISTRIBUTION** Throughout the island from lowlands to highlands. **BEHAVIOUR** Very little known in Sri Lanka. Most sightings are of solitary individuals. Probably has a social system like most cats, with males only pairing up for mating. Does not seem very shy. A Rusty-spotted Cat began visiting the Jetwing Vil Uyana hotel in Sigiriya soon after it was opened. Probably lives quite close to people in villages adjoining forests. Absent where good forests are not present. Climbs trees to hunt or rest, but most sightings are of cats patrolling on the ground. **DIET** Mainly small mammals such as mice and shrews, and birds. Known to raid hen houses.

Inhabits tall forests

Rusty spots on greyish-brown body and unmarked tail

Fishing Cat ■ *Prionailurus viverrina*

Large wild cat, with full-grown male growing to size of a dog. In other parts of its range in Southeast Asia, known to have taken children. Adults can be quite self-assured and fierce. Two white stripes extending up to forehead from eye. Two prominent white patches

on cheeks. Area around muzzle white on upper and lower jaws, a feature shared by the Rusty-spotted Cat (p. 95). Fur greyish with sides having blotches loosely forming longitudinal stripes. These are more distinct on dorsal area. Tail thick and lends appearance of cat being heavier at rear end. **HABITAT** Aquatic habitats bordered by suitable forest cover. Most lakes, ponds, canals and streams that have wooded areas harbour a population. **DISTRIBUTION** Lowlands to highlands, but absent from more northern parts of the island.

Two white stripes from forehead to eye

BEHAVIOUR A few people, including Anya Ratnayeke from the Small Cat Advocacy and Research, have been studying Fishing Cats in Colombo's wetland for several years and have used radio collars. Colombo is being branded the city of the Fishing Cat because of a well-established and widely distributed population in the many wetlands in and around the city. Unfortunately, as Colombo grows and fast-moving vehicular traffic continues throughout the night, the incidence of road kills is increasing. Mainly nocturnal in presence of people, but otherwise hunts by day. **DIET** Feeds on small animals and fish. Because of its size, most medium-sized animals are potential prey. **SUBSPECIES** Two subspecies recognized. *P. v. viverrinus* confined to Sri Lanka. *P. v. rizophoreus* has a curious disjunct distribution, being found in south-west India, at least two other localities in the Indian subcontinent at northerly latitudes, with a large area in between where it is absent, then extending down Southeast Asia and to some of the larger Indonesian islands such as Sumatra and Java.

Thick-set body

Leopard ▪ *Panthera pardus kotiya*

Top cat in Sri Lanka. Large spotted feline unlikely to be mistaken for any other animal. Melanistic or black leopards regularly reported, mainly from wet zone forests. Several factors contribute to good viewing of leopards in Sri Lanka in national parks such a Yala. The first is that it is the top predator. The second is its density – average density of leopards is so high because prey density is high. In sites such as Yala, this is a result of past human activities that have created a mosaic of grassland and scrub, and numerous waterholes. Protection from hunting (at least to a large degree) is a third factor. Fourthly, viewing is easy because of the park's terrain, comprising fairly short grassland and scrub, and plenty of rocky outcrops for leopards to climb up. **HABITAT & DISTRIBUTION** Once distributed throughout the whole island. Due to intense human activity, now extirpated from northern peninsula and populous western province. Wherever there is suitable forest cover, it continues to hold out. Comes to within a 100m of Nuwara Eliya town, which has beside it cloud forests of Mount Pedro Forest Range. Still holds out in forested ridges around town of Kandy. These and other leopards in the hills and highlands have been subject to a study by Andrew Kittle and Anjali Watson. **BEHAVIOUR** Like most cats, leopards use a single male to a multiple female social system. Size of a leopard's territory depends on availability of prey. In Yala, male's home range is 16–20km^2, encompassing home ranges of 3–4 females whose home ranges may be 2–4km^2. If, say, a mother with a home range of 3km^2 has two cubs, that would average one leopard per 1km^2. I have described in an article how one evening I watched six different leopards from a 600m length of road. Leopards scent mark their territories, enabling them to avoid actual physical combat that can be fatal to one or both combatants. Early in the morning or late in the evening, adults can be seen walking along dirt tracks and scent

Continued on p. 98.

Black rosettes on yellow body

marking. A rival leopard is able to gauge the sex and condition of another leopard from its scent marks. Young are termed cubs until around six months and subadults until about 18 months. At about 18 months, males are the size of the mother, and mother and cub are often mistaken for adult pair. In fact, most daytime sightings of leopards are of subadults. **DIET** Carnivorous, eating a range of mammals, from shrews and rodents to Water Buffalo. In national parks such as Yala, the Spotted Deer is preferred prey. In Horton Plains National Park, the Spotted Deer is absent but Sambar populations have grown in recent decades. Where leopards live close to people, they take domestic dogs and livestock, resulting in human-leopard conflict. **SUBSPECIES** Subspecies *kotiya* found in Sri Lanka has in the past been considered endemic to the island. Current thinking is that the 24 recognized subspecies can be reduced to just three, *pardus*, *fusca* and *saxicolor*, for all subspecies in Africa, Indian subcontinent and Central Asia. **WHERE TO SEE** Yala and Wilpattu national parks are very good. In the early 2000s, I began to publicize that Sri Lanka is the most reliable place in the world in which to see a leopard. Initially, many in the tourism industry were sceptical of my claims. Now, Yala National Park has visitor-management issues with visitors wanting to see leopards. It is clear that Yala may need to be zoned to provide a zone at a lower fee for affordability and for those whom leopards may not be the principal focus, while having a premium zone for those who prefer an area where the number of vehicles is restricted.

Long tail and graceful build

VIVERRIDAE (CIVETS & PALM CIVETS)

The viverrids comprise the genets, civets and oyans (the superficially similar mongooses are in the family Herpestidae), and are among the three largest carnivore families, distributed in the Old World tropics (Africa and Asia). The Common Genet *Genetta genetta*, found in southern Europe, may be an introduction. The family has 34 plus species in 14 genera. Two of the four subfamilies are found in Sri Lanka.

The subfamily Viverrinae is represented by one species in Sri Lanka – the Small Indian Civet. Civets are cat-like nocturnal animals that prefer to hunt on the ground, although they are good climbers. The subfamily Paradoxurinae has four species in Sri Lanka, including the endemic Golden Palm Civet, which is now split into three species. However, Vernon et. al. (2015) argue that the variation seen in Sri Lanka is normal and does not support the split into three species. Palm civets are arboreal and nocturnal.

Scent plays a very important role in communication with the viverrids, with vocalizations being limited to a few bird-like yelps. All of the viverrids have well-developed anal glands that are used to deposit scent marks in their territories.

Common Palm Civet ▪ *Paradoxurus hermaphroditus*

(Toddy Cat)

Common, but many people do not see it because of its nocturnal habits. When seen in the dark, can seem jet-black; in fact fur is more greyish than black and seems to fit somewhat loosely on its body. Long bodied and long tailed, with short feet. Pale patch on face to break up its outline, a feature common in many nocturnal mammals. **HABITAT** Needs wooded patches in the wild. In urban areas has adapted to well-wooded home gardens, even in the heart of big cities such as Colombo. **DISTRIBUTION** Throughout the island. **BEHAVIOUR** Usually seen singly. Young seem to be taken care of by mother, with 3–4 in a litter; they utter bird-like, twittering calls. In the wild sleeps and breed in tree holes or crevices in rocky outcrops. In

Continued on p. 100.

May shelter indoors in urban areas

cities seems perfectly happy to find a dry corner under a roof. My house in Colombo 8 has palm civets that take up residence from time to time. They make their presence felt when they bound across roofs and jump from one level to another, landing with a loud thud. I once watched a mother jump about two body lengths across from one roof to another with a youngster held in her mouth. Can shuffle backwards in a straight line without any difficulty – probably an adaptation enabling them to reverse out of tree holes and rock crevices, which they investigate in search of food. **DIET** Wide variety of food, including small mammals such as rats and mice, insects and fruits. Often seen climbing to tops of fruiting trees to feed on fruits. Its droppings, often found strewn on rocks and logs, may contain partly digested seeds of the *kithul* tree *Caryota urens*. Said to be fond of stealing juice of trees, which is 'tapped', hence the local name Toddy Cat.

Pale face-patches for disruptive camouflage

Wet Zone Golden Palm Civet ■ *Paradoxurus aureus*

The golden palm civet species are not likely to be confused with the Common Palm Civet (p. 99) because of their uniform reddish or brownish colour. Slightly smaller and less common than Common. Overlooked because of its arboreal habits. On a night walk in a forested area, it will not be seen unless a torch beam (use a weak red light) is shone on to crowns of tall trees. I have found it to be fairly self-assured when it is on a tree, often watching an observer calmly and seeming to be in no hurry to move away. **HABITAT** Tall forests. Does not appear averse to occupying tall trees close to human habitation, but absent from areas where large forest stretches are no longer available. **DISTRIBUTION** Wet lowlands to mid-hills. **BEHAVIOUR** Often seen singly or in pairs. Seems to live all its life up in trees. Not very vocal. Sleeps in tree hole. **DIET** Mix of fruits, including berries, and small animals such as birds, lizards, amphibians and insects. Main food probably consists of native fruits, although it visits home gardens to feed on jak, mango, bananas and the like. **WHERE TO SEE** Tall forests around Martin's Simple Lodge in Sinharaja.

Uniform body colour

Dry Zone Golden Palm Civet ▪ *Paradoxurus stenocephalus*

Colin Groves and others, in a paper published in 2009, suggested that the Golden Palm Civet is actually four species: the Wet Zone Golden Palm Civet *P. aureus*, Montane Golden Palm Civet (Sri Lanka Brown Palm Civet) *P. montanus*, Dry Zone Golden Palm Civet *P. stenocephalus* and another yet to be described species. The species-level distinctions are based on subtle measurements of skulls and other body parts. The rare

photographs included here are of the Dry Zone Golden Palm Civet, taken in Wilpattu by day. As can be seen, its colour is brown. **HABITAT** Probably widespread in dry monsoon forests. **DISTRIBUTION** Probably widespread in dry lowlands. Likely more common than records suggest because not much attention has been paid to it. **BEHAVIOUR AND DIET** Probably similar to the Wet Zone Golden Palm Civet's (p. 101). **WHERE TO SEE** I have seen it at dusk in the forests surrounding Sigiriya Moat.

Uniform brown colouration

Dry zone species may be just a colour variant of a single species

Small Indian Civet ■ *Viverricula indica*

(Ring-tailed Civet)

Unmistakable, with black and white body, and tail with black and white rings. One of the more common nocturnal animals seen when driving at night along forested roads in the country. **HABITAT** Forests, but has become habituated and visits houses and explores dustbins for food. Quite a few bungalows inside national parks have a regular civet that will come in and turn over the bin to look for scraps of food. It is, however, much shyer of people than the Common Palm Civet (p. 99), which may take up residence in the roofs of houses. **DISTRIBUTION** Throughout the island, from lowlands to highlands. **BEHAVIOUR** Usually seen singly. Like all civets and palm civets, marks territory with droppings on exposed rocks and tree trunks. Often seen hunting on the ground, although equally comfortable climbing trees in pursuit of prey. **DIET** Favours hunting for small mammals such as rodents, hares and mouse-deer. Also eats fruits, including berries, and roots. More carnivorous than palm civets found in Sri Lanka. I have seen it eating freshly hatched termites emerging from the ground. **WHERE TO SEE** Often seen on night drives on public roads running through forested areas. Around midnight, when traffic is at its lowest, is the best chance to see it. A night walk outside many of Sri Lanka's hotels, which have well-wooded grounds, provides a chance of seeing one.

Distinctive black rings on tail

HERPESTIDAE (MONGOOSES)
Mongooses have traditionally been placed in the Viverridae family with the genets and civets. Recent molecular studies have supported the view that they should be placed in their own family. In fact, molecular work shows that they are closer to the hyaenas (Hyaenidae family) than the civets. The Herpestidae comprises two subfamilies, the Mungotinae, the social mongooses with 11 species, which are absent from Sri Lanka, and the Herpestinae with 23 species in nine genera. Of the latter, one genus, *Herpestes*, is present in Sri Lanka, with four species. A skull of a mongoose in the genus *Herpestes* dating to 30 million years ago shows this to be one of the oldest carnivore genera. All of Sri Lanka's mongooses are in this genus and in a sense they are almost living fossils. They are short legged, long bodied and not cat-like. They are mainly diurnal and likely to be seen easily by visitors to wilderness areas.

Indian Grey Mongoose ▪ *Herpestes edwardsii*

Easily identified by uniform grizzled grey hue without any contrasting markings. Smaller than other mongooses. Eyes reddish. **HABITAT** Grassland and grassy verges, and lightly wooded country. **DISTRIBUTION** Throughout the island, but most common northwards

Grizzled grey fur

Reddish eyes

from north-central province. In cultural triangle area of dry lowlands it is impossible to drive around for a day without seeing one; by contrast it is very scarce in south. I have had just a handful of sightings despite a few hundred game drives in Yala National Park. **BEHAVIOUR** Tends to be solitary although at times pairs are seen. Very wary, and usually dashes across a road. At certain places like the moat at Sigiriya, has become accustomed to humans and may sit on a wall sunning itself. However, if you stop and point a camera at it, more often than not it will feel ill at ease with the attention and move away. Very diurnal in its habits. **DIET** Omnivorous. Takes fruits, including berries, and roots. However, prefers animals from invertebrates to small rodents. **WHERE TO SEE** The moat around Sigiriya early in the morning is a good place to find one on the prowl. Otherwise, you can see it dashing across roads when visiting cultural sites in north-central province.

Indian Brown Mongoose ▪ *Herpestes fuscus*

Can only be confused with the Ruddy Mongoose (opposite). Separated from Ruddy by lack of black tip to tail, and end of tail not being carried in upturned manner. Coat also

lacks 'grizzled' appearance of Ruddy, which shows at close quarters. Unlike Ruddy, which has become fairly tolerant to safari vehicles in national parks, Indian Brown and Indian Grey Mongooses (p. 104) remain very wary and take flight if you stop to pay them any attention. I have seen this species playing in my garden by day, but it would bolt out of sight if I ventured out with a camera. One of the hardest mammals to photograph, although found in even the most densely inhabited cities. **HABITAT** Very adaptable and can live in the heart of Colombo as well as in densely

wooded forests. **DISTRIBUTION** Throughout the island to highlands. **BEHAVIOUR** Usually solitary. Can be active by day. In places where it is not persecuted, visits rubbish dumps during daylight. However, seems more comfortable at night. **DIET** Omnivorous, taking fruits, including berries, occasionally. Mainstay of diet is animals ranging from worms and grubs, to small mammals such as rodents and hares.

Rufous fur; tail held horizontally, and with no black tip

Ruddy Mongoose ■ *Herpestes smithii*

Common mongoose in lowlands in southern half of the island. May be confused with the Indian Brown Mongoose (opposite), which also has uniformly brown colouration on body and tail. Ruddy can always be separated by black tip to tail. It is also 'rude', carrying its tail curled up as if 'giving you the finger'. **HABITAT** Forested areas. **DISTRIBUTION** Throughout the island in forested areas. In north displaced by the Indian Grey Mongoose (p. 104) and in west by Indian Brown. However, I have once photographed the Ruddy in Sinharaja. **BEHAVIOUR** Often in pairs. Somewhat shy, tending to melt into forest when encountered on a game drive, although sometimes a pair will walk nonchalantly past a parked safari vehicle. Seen by day in national parks such as Yala and Wilpattu. Good climber but this is not readily apparent – in most encounters, likely to be seen walking on the ground. **DIET** Carnivorous. Also scavenges kills of other animals. Common visitor to kills made by leopards.

Tail points up

Distinctive black tip to tail

Stripe-necked Mongoose ■ *Herpestes vitticollis*

Large mongoose, distinctive with black stripe on neck, starting from behind ear and extending towards top of forelegs. Largest mongoose in Asia. Thick, fluffy tail has long black tip. Mature adults have grey on head and rusty-brown diffuse band around rump. Legs black. No other mongoose in Sri Lanka is as colourful. **HABITAT** Seldom seen away from forests. Most common in dry zone forests. **DISTRIBUTION** Throughout the island up to Horton Plains National Park. Scarce in northern part of the island. **BEHAVIOUR** May be seen in pairs or singly. Sightings can be variable. On some visits to Yala National Park I have not had even one sighting, but on others I have had one on at least one of every two game drives. I have often watched a pair digging in soft, damp soil or sandy soil to ferret out grubs. Outside national parks, extremely shy and almost impossible to see. Largely

Black ear-stripe

diurnal. **DIET** Omnivorous. Eats fruits, including berries, and roots. Due to large size, also hunts small mammals such as mouse-deer and hares. Also eats birds, bird's eggs, and invertebrates and their larvae. **SUBSPECIES** Species found only in southern India and Sri Lanka. One subspecies confined to Uttara Kannada (previously North Kanara) in India. Subspecies *H. v. vitticollis* found in rest of its range in southern India and Sri Lanka. **WHERE TO SEE** Yala a reliable site and probably best location in which to see this beautiful animal. However, even in Yala, 10 game drives may be needed before it is seen. Seen less often at Horton Plains, where it tends to keep a fair distance from people.

Multi-coloured body

Canidae (Dogs)

Native dog, or canid, species are found on all continents except Antarctica. They occupy every terrestrial habitat, from desert, rainforest and mountain steppe, to the icy Arctic, and are the most widespread carnivore family. They have triangular faces with pointed muzzles and large ears. The typical 'dog face' is familiar since the domestic dog is descended from the wolf. About 35 species are recognized in 13 genera. Sri Lanka has only one species – the Golden Jackal, which in earlier books is referred to as the Black-backed Jackal. It is found on three continents (in southern Europe, the northern half of Africa, and across the Middle East to Asia), but is not as widespread as the Red Fox *Vulpes vulpes*, the most widespread carnivore in the world. Canids are highly intelligent and affectionate, forming close social bonds. They are generally omnivorous, but prefer to take vertebrate animals for prey. Canid diversity is highest in Sudan, with 10 species, and the USA with nine species. Most canids actively scent mark territories using both dung and urine.

Golden Jackal ▪ *Canis aureus*

Next to the leopard and crocodile, the Golden Jackal is probably the most important high-level carnivore, regulating prey populations in lowland jungles, especially in the dry zone. In older books Sri Lankan subspecies *lankae* is known as the Black-backed Jackal (a

Continued on p. 110.

Grey-black back on Sri Lankan endemic subspecies

name now used for another species). Looks noticeably different from the Golden Jackal of mainland India. **HABITAT** Hunts in open habitats such as grassland, as well as scrub forest. **DISTRIBUTION** Throughout the island, but less so in higher mountains. Still holds out in extensive areas of marshland such as at Muthurajawela, about 20km north of Colombo, and still seen even closer to Colombo in areas adjoining Bolgoda Lake. **BEHAVIOUR** Hunts in small packs, although quite often seen in pairs. Interesting social structure, in which alpha pair breeds and others in pack are 'helpers', which may benefit by learning skills of parenthood. In national parks in dry zone, may be seen at almost any time, although more likely to lie up in shaded thicket during heat of the day. Rukshan Jayewardene, a wildlife photographer, wrote of an encounter where a leopard attacked a jackal. It feigned death, tricking the leopard, which let down its guard, allowing the jackal to get away. **DIET** Omnivorous. Wide diet, from lizards, birds and small mammals, to scavenging on dead animals. When animals are scarce, also eat fruits, including berries.

Wild canids have forwards-facing eyes and pointed muzzles

> **URSIDAE (BEARS)**
> Bears are found across northern latitudes extending down the USA to South America, as well as in southern Europe, south Asia, and Southeast Asia and the Indonesian islands, occupying a wide range of habitats, from the Arctic to dry and wet forests. They are absent from the Middle East, Africa and Australia. Characterized by big heads and thick necks that merge into a rotund body, they have relatively small eyes and lack whiskers. There are eight species in five genera. Sri Lanka has one species, which is endemic to south Asia. Bears are grouped into three subfamilies, with the Giant Panda (subfamily Ailuropodinae) and Andean Bear (subfamily Trematctinae) being the only members of their subfamilies. The other six species are in the subfamily Ursinae, which has three genera. Bears are omnivorous, eating a wide range of plant and animal matter. They are believed to have evolved from canids (dogs). The Red Panda is not a bear and is unrelated to the Giant Panda. Bears are not very vocal and scent mark to communicate. In northern latitudes bears hibernate during winter.

Sloth Bear ▪ *Melursus ursinus*

Characterized by long, powerful claws and uneven black fur that can look patchy on many adults. Long, pale muzzle. The only bear species on the island. Bears are among the most dangerous of animals to encounter, and some villagers have had their faces badly mauled in a bear attack. Often attacks heads of victims, sometimes rearing up on hind legs to do so. **DISTRIBUTION** Throughout dry lowlands. Distribution does not coincide with distribution of termites, one of its favorite foods. It is a puzzle as to why it is absent from wet zone. In the past, known to make movements up into hills in search of food during times of extreme drought. **BEHAVIOUR** Usually seen singly. It would seem males part company with females after mating. Females often seen with young, usually two and at times three. The bears may, however, spend the day in communal sleeping sites. On one occasion I came across a mother lying on her back with her feet in the air and a cub on the soles of her feet. I could almost imagine her juggling the infant. As my jeep came around the bend, she got on to her feet, one of the cubs clambered on to her back for a ride, and the family vanished. Bears are not territorial and males and females share home ranges with other male or female bears. Outside national parks such as Yala and Wilpattu, it is almost impossible to see a Sloth Bear, because they are nocturnal. Wasgomuwa National Park is reputed to have the highest density. Radio-collar studies

Long, pale muzzle

Continued on p. 112.

Claws can rip termite nests

in Wasgomuwa by Shyamala Ratnayeke have shed more light on the social behaviour of Sloth Bears. They found that males and females had home ranges of 2.2 and 3.8km² respectively. There was also considerable overlap between the home ranges within and between sexes. **DIET** Like all bears, can vary diet according to availability of food and eats wide range of plant and animal matter. However, this species is on the evolutionary road to semi-specialization and has lost a few front teeth to enable it to purse its lips and create a suction pump to suck in termites. Powerful claws enable it to rip down strong termite mounds of baked mud to feed on termites. During dry season, when termite mounds are as hard as concrete, switches to fruits, including berries, grubs and other insects. Does not normally actively hunt animals but happily steals from kills of other carnivores. Fruits of the *palu*, or Ceylon Ironwood *Manilkara hexandra*, are a favourite during July when the trees are in fruit. **WHERE TO SEE** Yala and Wilpattu National Parks are best options year round. July, when *palu* is in fruit, is an especially good time for daytime sightings. The bears become inebriated after gorging themselves on fruits. I once watched one come down a tree in a drunken swagger, and collide with the tyre of a parked vehicle.

Blunt muzzle, and long body on short feet

> **MUSTELLIDAE (WEASELS, OTTERS & ALLIES)**
> The mustelids have a wide geographical distribution, with native species almost everywhere and notable absences in Australia, New Guinea and New Zealand. With 57 species spread across 22 genera, the mustelids are the largest of the carnivore families. They are small to medium-sized mammals with bushy tails. Modern taxonomists recognize eight subfamilies within this complex family, including otters (Lutrinae). The Lutrinae subfamily contains seven genera and 12 species in three lineages: the Giant Otter, New World otters (four *Lontra* species) and Old World otters (five genera). The Eurasian Otter is the only mustelid found in Sri Lanka. Otters are adapted to swimming and hunting in aquatic environments. They are very active, never seeming to sit still. Fish form an important part of their diet, although they readily take other aquatic animals. The widespread Eurasian Otter has a disjunct distribution in south Asia, being largely absent across most of India, but present in south India and Sri Lanka.

Eurasian Otter ■ *Lutra lutra*

Enigmatic animal, with many Sri Lankans probably not even aware off its presence in Sri Lanka. Appears a little awkward on land because of its short feet. Feet webbed – an adaptation for aquatic hunting. Thick, sausage-like body with tail thick at base. Uniformly chocolate-brown on upperparts and pale underneath. Very graceful in water.
HABITAT Wherever unpolluted streams, rivers, ponds and lakes occur throughout the island. On a visit to Mannar Island, I saw one crossing a busy main road in the town near Medawachchiya. However, it only passes through urban areas and only settles down where there is a quite wide extent of natural green area together with clean water. Holds out in suburbs of Colombo, which still has sizeable fragments of a once-extensive network of wetlands.
DISTRIBUTION Throughout the island. I have seen it in the

Continued on p. 114.

Uniform chocolate-brown on upperparts

'Arrenga Pool' at Horton Plains National Park. **BEHAVIOUR** Although I have had a few daytime sightings, it is largely nocturnal, perhaps due to predation pressures from domestic dogs and persecution from humans who may mistake it for a mongoose, which kills domestic poultry. **DIET** Fish a large part of diet, but also eats a range of aquatic animals, from invertebrates such as molluscs and freshwater crabs, to amphibians. Being a sizeable carnivore, will also eat small mammals such as rodents, and waterbirds, if the opportunity presents itself.

Thick body pale underneath

SUIDAE (PIGS)

Pigs are familiar mammals with a rotund body, bristly coat, short legs, and large, elongated head with an unusual nose ending in a broad, flat, oval-shaped disc. Many species have long canines that extend outwards. These tusks are used for fighting with males of the same species, and in defensive aggression against predators. The family extends from Western Europe to east Asia. It is absent across a broad belt of northern Africa, but widespread in the lower two-thirds of the continent. There are 17 species in six genera. The species found in Sri Lanka is the same one that was once extirpated from Britain but has now re-established feral colonies from escapees. About 18 subspecies of the Eurasian Wild Pig are recognized, with the subspecies *affinis* distributed in south India and Sri Lanka. The genus *Sus* has seven species, of which six are found only in Asia.

Eurasian Wild Pig ▪ *Sus scrofa*

Generally very shy animal because it is hunted for its meat. In protected areas such as bigger national parks in dry lowlands, it is more confiding and at times gathers into herds or sounders numbering more than 30 individuals. At game lodges, becomes quite bold. Boars are potentially quite dangerous as they can inflict heavy damage with their tusks. They readily take on a leopard that threatens a herd. I once observed a sounder that was stalked by a leopard. The young and adult females quickly gathered into a creche, with adult males

Continued on p. 116.

Juveniles have pale stripes

Large, elongated head with flat nose

throwing a defensive ring around them. Four adult males then approached the leopard, which fled up a tree. The males stood guard for a while, while the females and young moved away. **HABITAT** Occurs in large herds in national parks in dry lowlands. Small herds or solitary animals found in wet zone forests. **DISTRIBUTION** Throughout the island to highlands wherever dry zone scrub or wet zone forest provides cover. **BEHAVIOUR** Males develop formidable tusks that can inflict heavy damage on a hunter. Adult males often seen alone and probably join herds of females and young only to breed. **DIET** Omnivorous. Causes much damage to home gardens and plantations by uprooting plants for rhizomes. Readily scavenges meat. I once came across a herd tearing apart and eating a Spotted Deer fawn. How the fawn died was not clear.

Elongated canines can inflict heavy injuries

> ### TRAGULIDAE (CHEVROTAINS)
> Two chevrotain species are presently recognized in Sri Lanka, the White-spotted Mouse-deer and Yellow-striped Mouse-deer. I have retained the old name mouse-deer rather than the more correct name chevrotain because in Sri Lanka everyone refers to them as mouse-deer. Groves & Meijaard in 2005 proposed splitting into two species what had hitherto been described as one species. The species found in India, which was considered the same species as in Sri Lanka, is now considered a distinct species: the Indian Mouse-deer *Moschiola indica*. Elsewhere in Southeast Asia there are five species in the genus *Tragulus*. Africa has just one chevrotain – the African or Water Chevrotain *Hyemoschus aquaticus*, known for its aquatic behaviour, which has also been observed in Asian chevrotains.
>
> Chevrotains in the Tragulidae family are considered an ancient group going back to the Miocene Epoch. They are thought to be an early offshoot of the Ruminantia. A chevrotain-like animal in the genus *Indohyus*, existing 48 million years ago, is considered a missing link between ungulates and modern-day whales. Chevrotains are not true tree climbers, but are able to clamber up trees that are at a slant and covered in creepers. They do so to escape from terrestrial predators such as dogs. They are not very vocal, but give a bark-like call when alarmed. The males develop elongated canines.

White-spotted
Mouse-deer ▪ *Moschiola meminna*

The Indian Mouse-deer M. *indica* is described by Groves & Meijaard (2005) as having upper row of spots forming continuous stripe on shoulder, but breaking down into spots halfway along body. The White-spotted Mouse-deer of Sri Lanka is recognized by upper row of spots not fusing to form continuous stripe even on shoulder. Colour of Indian and White-spotted dull brown. **HABITAT & DISTRIBUTION** Dry zone scrub forests of Sri Lanka. Has adapted to home gardens in villages. **BEHAVIOUR** Usually seen singly or in pairs. Largely nocturnal in behaviour, but I have seen it active by day inside national parks. **DIET** Feeds on grasses, herbaceous plants, tender leaves and fallen fruits, including berries. **WHERE TO SEE** National parks such as Yala and Wilpattu may occasionally yield a sighting as one dashes across the road.

Upper row of spots forms continuous shoulder-stripe

Yellow-striped Mouse-deer ■ *Moschiola kathygre*

Groves & Meijaard (2005) describe colour as being more ochre-brown and warmer than in other species. Spots and stripes more yellowy than white. Two longitudinal rows

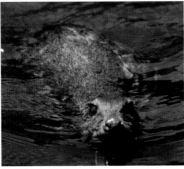

of elongated spots on flanks fused into 'tolerably complete longitudinal stripes', with elongated spot row between them and two more spot rows above them. **HABITAT & DISTRIBUTION** Wet zone to mid-hills. Range extends in south-east to Kataragama in Yala, where dry zone species, the White-spotted Mouse-deer (p. 117) is present. Often also seeks refuge in home gardens. **BEHAVIOUR** Usually seen singly or in pairs. **DIET** Feeds on grasses, herbaceous plants, tender leaves and fallen fruits, including berries. Probably plays a role in thinning out emergence of new forest plants under mother trees.

Aquatic escape behaviour

Spots and stripes yellowy rather than white

CERVIDAE (DEER)
Fifty-three species of deer in 18 genera are found in North and South America, Europe, the Middle East and Asia. Deer are notably absent from Africa, Australia and surrounding islands such as New Guinea and New Zealand. The similar looking antelopes and gazelles in Africa are in another family, the bovines (Bovidae). which includes cattle. The Cervidae comprises two subfamilies; the Cervinae and Capreolinae. The latter, which is absent from Sri Lanka, comprises three tribes containing the roe deer (Capreolini), moose (Alceini) and New World deer (Odocoileini). The subfamily found in Sri Lanka consists of the tribe Muntiacini, which contains 12 muntjac species, and Cervini, which has 18 species of Old World deer. The deer are characterized by an elongated head on a stockily built neck and a short tail. They occupy a range of habitats from the Arctic tundra to dense forest.

Sri Lanka has four deer species in the family Cervidae. Of these, it is not clear whether the Hog Deer is native or if it was introduced. It is restricted to coastal swampland in the south-west. Male deer adopt a harem system and develop impressive antlers. During growth, these are covered with blood vessels and the deer are referred to as being in velvet. I have seen deer nibbling shed antlers, perhaps to ingest calcium and other minerals.

The Spotted Deer and Sambar employ a harem system. Muntjacs are usually found solitarily or in pairs. Deer have glands in front of their eyes (anteorbital) that they use to scent mark trees and other vegetation. They can also be quite vocal. Muntjac have pronounced facial glands and scent marking may play a stronger role in maintaining pair bonds and territories in these deer than in others.

Spotted Deer ■ *Axis axis*

(Chital)
Deer species most likely to be seen by visitors to national parks. Often found in association with Hanuman Langurs (p. 23), with which it seems to have a symbiotic relationship. The two species probably assist each other with enhanced vigilance, and the deer may gain some extra foraging benefit from the foliage broken by the langurs. **HABITAT** Needs grassy glades for grazing and forest cover for shade during heat of the day. Found in scrub jungles of dry lowlands. **DISTRIBUTION** Where suitable dry zone scrub forest is present, except in northern peninsula. Because of poaching, now virtually confined

Stag in velvet

Continued on p. 120.

Female with fawn

to protected areas. Outside protected areas nocturnal in habit. **BEHAVIOUR** Occurs in herds. Males challenge each other during the rut to take control of a harem of females. One dominant male typically secures mating rights to group of females. However, mixed herds are quite often seen with several males mingling with females. Stags at times 'decorate' their antlers with vegetation for displaying. Only males develop antlers. **DIET** Herbivorous. Occasionally browses on low-hanging branches, but feeds mainly by grazing on grass.

Only males develop antlers

Hog Deer ■ *Axis porcinus*

Superficially looks like small version of the Sambar (p. 122), but about half the size. Back rises up to elevated rump. Also carries itself differently. Males a third bigger than females. **HABITAT** Found in swampland and paddy fields fringed with cover in south-west of the island. Injured animals are sometimes brought to Hiyare Research Centre near Galle. **DISTRIBUTION** Curiously disjunct distribution, with nearest population being in north of India in Himalayan foothills. Was found across Southeast Asia to China, but has become locally extinct in many countries due to habitat conversion. Disjunct distribution has led to speculation that it may have been introduced to Sri Lanka, but there is no record of when, why and by whom. **BEHAVIOUR** Mainly solitary unless a mother is with young. Hardly seen in the wild because of nocturnal feeding. Nocturnal behaviour may be driven by risk of opportunistic poaching. **DIET** Mainly feeds on aquatic herbs and other water-loving herbaceous plants.

caption

Females lack antlers

Sambar ■ *Rusa unicolor*

Largest deer in the island. Easily identified by uniform, dark chocolate-brown colour and large size. Sadly remains a popular quarry of poachers and is extremely wary, even in national parks and reserves. The one exception is Horton Plains National Park – the only place in Sri Lanka where Sambar are seen in herds of any size. There are two reasons for this. One is the presence of large grasslands, the nutritional content of which is artificially high due to escape of an introduced grass species a few decades ago from nearby Ambewela cattle farm. The other reason is the protection offered with the permanent presence of rangers and regular visitation by the public. **HABITAT** Can occupy wide range of habitats, from dense rainforests to open grassland. However, always needs cover of wooded thickets

Adult males develop seasonal antlers and shaggy neck

for lying up by day. **DISTRIBUTION** Throughout the island wherever sizeable pockets of forest and grassland remain. Populations of any significant numbers increasingly confined to protected areas. **BEHAVIOUR** Only males develop antlers. They battle for control of harems of females, similarly to other deer species such as the Spotted Deer (p. 119), which inhabits open country. Main predator is the leopard, although young may be taken by jackals. In dry lowlands, wary of crocodiles when drinking. Even in Horton Plains, where it has become habituated, more active by night. By the evening, sizeable herds of up to 30 may gather in the open to forage on grass. In forested areas stags may only associate with females during rutting season. Males often bellow to establish their territorial dominance, and also give a short, sharp bark when alarmed. The far-carrying bark often alerts other animals to the presence of a predator such as a leopard. **DIET** Herbivorous. Being a forest deer, mainly a browser, feeding on leaves and shoots of plants. Also grazes on grasses. **WHERE TO SEE** Sightings guaranteed in the evenings in Horton Plains National Park.

Short tail

Red Muntjac ■ *Muntiacus muntjak*

(Barking Deer)

Uniformly brown, medium-sized deer with small antlers mounted on long pedicles. Often seen singly, one prominent exception being in Wilpattu National Park, where small groups can gather. Generally thinly distributed. **HABITAT** Favours areas where forest cover is interspersed with grassland. Habitat at Wilpattu is ideal. Many highland patana grasslands with ridge-top forest also provide a preferred habitat. **DISTRIBUTION** Throughout lowlands to highlands, but less abundant in highest elevations. Nevertheless, at times in the early morning, small numbers can be seen grazing on agricultural fields bordering cloud forests close to Horton Plains National Park. Phillips (1980) states that its range south-

east extends into Ruhunu (Yala) National Park, but I have never seen it there. At least nine subspecies are recognized, and the Red Muntjac is found from India and Sri Lanka, to Southeast Asia, extending to Borneo, Java and Sumatra. **BEHAVIOUR** Usually occurs singly or in pairs, but where not hunted forms small groups. Due to hunting has become wary and nocturnal in most areas. Best clue to its presence is a barking call, usually uttered in alarm or when bucks are in rut. Canine teeth developed into tushes (small, tusk-like protrusions). These are used in defence and can inflict serious damage on predators. **DIET** Forages on succulent grasses and tender leaves.

Males have simple antlers and elongated canines

Bovidae (Hollow-horned Ruminants)

This family comprises 279 species in 54 genera, and is the largest and most diverse family in the order Artiodactyla, or even-toed ungulates. It is absent from South America and Australia and the large islands of New Guinea and New Zealand. There are two main subfamilies: the Bovinae with three tribes and the Antilopinae with nine tribes, with the latter absent from Sri Lanka. The Bovinae comprises three tribes: cattle and Water Buffalo (Bovini), Nilgai and Chowsingha (Boselaphini), and Bushbuck, kudus and Eland (Tragelaphini). The only member of the family occurring in a wild state in Sri Lanka is the Water Buffalo, although it is possible that the animals found in the wild may owe their origins to animals imported in the distant past. In many ruminants the horns are circular in cross-section, although this is not the case in Water Buffaloes.

Water Buffalo ■ *Bubalus bubalis*

Not likely to be confused with any other mammal in Sri Lanka and the only bovine family member occurring in a wild state. There is debate as to whether wild Water Buffalos are truly native or whether they originate from imported domestic animals that have been

Continued on p. 126.

wild for several hundred years. Most probably they are descendants of imported animals – original range of wild Water Buffalo was in Nepalese terai, plains of the Ganges and Brahmaputra in Assam. I have heard accounts of people passing a submerged bull for it to emerge from the water and gore the walker from behind. In remote areas, people die from internal bleeding before they can be treated. **HABITAT** Scrub forest with grassland and waterholes in dry lowlands. **DISTRIBUTION** In the wild, almost entirely restricted to national parks in dry lowlands. **BEHAVIOUR** Fairly close-knit structure. When herd is moving, hierarchy and sex of individual determines its relative position in herd. Dominant male may at times follow behind another adult male, which takes a 'pathfinder' position. Does not generally defend a territory as such, but does have home range in which it moves around. **DIET** Browses on aquatic plants. Grazes short grassland.

Adult male

MARINE MAMMALS

Three scientific orders of marine mammal have been recorded in Sri Lanka, the Sirenia, Carnivora and Cetacea. Two have a regular presence in Sri Lanka – the Sirenia with the Dugong, and the Cetacea with the whales and dolphins. A juvenile Southern Elephant Seal – an earless seal of a family in the Carnivora order – strayed on to the west coast of Sri Lanka in November 2019. The three marine mammal orders covered here are not closely related, but are grouped together for practical convenience.

DUGONGIDAE (DUGONG)

The order Sirenia comprises two families, the Trichechidae (manatees) and Dugongidae (Dugong). There are three manatee species in a single genus, found in the Amercias and West Africa. They have rounded and fan-shaped (or paddle-shaped) tail fins. The Dugongidae has just one species, the Dugong, found from the eastern shoreline of Africa across the Middle East and Asia, to the northern coastlines of Australia, and to the islands north of it including the Sunda and Philippine Islands, and New Guinea.

Dugong ▪ *Dugong dugon*

Relatively small, greyish marine mammal. On surfacing, blow not conspicuous as in marine mammals like whales, so is easily missed. 'Fish-tail', or 'whale-tail', easily separates

Continued on p. 128.

Dugongs rarely betray their presence when they surface

Seagrass, food for Dugongs

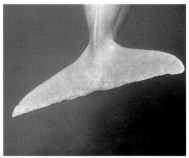

Straight trailing edge

it from manatees, which have rounded, fan-shaped tails and are not found in Indian Ocean. Dorsal fin absent. Muzzle directed facing downwards and forms flat, horseshoe-shaped disc, making it easier to feed on sea bottom. Small black eye, with no eyelashes on eyelid. **HABITAT** Seagrass beds. **DISTRIBUTION** Seagrass beds are found in warm, shallow waters, so known mainly from Mannar Basin, from Kalpitiya Peninsula to Adam's Bridge stretch of islands, in north-west Sri Lanka. Very rare now. Reduction in numbers could be mainly due to hunting and accidental bycatch, together with changes that could have led to reductions in the seagrass beds that it is dependent on. **BEHAVIOUR** Occasionally forms small herds that are transient. Typically goes about individually, sometime swimming a few hundred kilometres to reach seagrass beds. Sleeps by day and grazes on seagrass at night. Reported to be wary of humans, which may be due to being hunted for food, although it is legally protected. Recorded to live up to 73 years. **DIET** Mainly seagrasses but also algae and seabed invertebrates, including clams and worms.

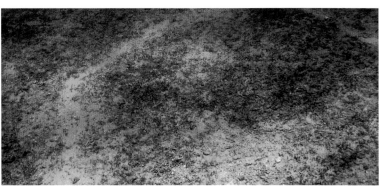

Dugong feeding trails

> **PHOCIDAE (EARLESS SEALS)**
> This family has 18 species in 13 genera, mainly in temperate and high latitudes. Nine species are found in northern latitudes in temperate and polar waters, with four species confined to Antarctica's Southern Ocean. Two species are confined to fresh water in the Baikal and Caspian Sea respectively. Earless seals, together with eared seals (family Otariide) and the Walrus (family Odobenidae) were once grouped in their own order, the Pinnipedia, but have since been demoted to a suborder of the Carnivora.

Southern Elephant Seal ▪ *Mirounga leonina*

On 20 November 2019, on Dalawella Beach, near Unawatuna, close to the whale-watching port of Mirissa on Sri Lanka's south coast, the navy observed a juvenile seal that was widely reported in the press. A Southern Elephant Seal had arrived in Sri Lankan waters for the first time, and crowds of onlookers gathered at two beaches (Dalawella and later Kollupitiya in Colombo) to view it when it came ashore to rest. The visiting

Continued on p. 130.

The exhausted juvenile that arrived in Sri Lanka (juveniles have flat faces)

seal added a new family, the Phocidae, to the Sri Lankan mammal fauna. The dark seal in the photograph below is the juvenile that arrived in Sri Lanka, photographed by Riaz Cader, and the adult with the inflated nose and pup are from images taken in Antarctica. Juveniles have flat faces and large dark eyes, and a uniformly coloured coat. **DISTRIBUTION** Breeding sites are on subantarctic islands, Antarctic peninsula and coast of Argentina. **BEHAVIOUR** Known to forage over vast distances at sea and to dive to depths of 400–800m. A few previous records of them having reached tropical waters. Males bigger than females and guard harems during breeding season. Males have inflatable noses. Solitary at sea but gathers in large colonies for moulting and breeding. **DIET** Mainly fish and squid. Feeding dives last 20–30 minutes.

Pup (Antarctica)

Juvenile (Sri Lanka)

Adult males develop inflated noses (Antarctica)

CETACEA

The order Cetacea, comprising the whales, porpoises and dolphins, consists of three suborders. The Archaeoceti is an extinct suborder known from fossils. The two living suborders are the Mysticeti (baleen whales), and Odontoceti (toothed whales), with the two suborders comprising 14 families and 90 species.

The Mysticeti have sheets of baleen in their mouths that they use for sieving food. The Odontoceti have teeth. The Mysticeti have two external blowholes. Although the Odontoceti have only one external blowhole, internally they have two nasal passages, like the baleen whales.

The baleen whales include the family Balaenopteridae (rorqual whales), which have numerous ventral grooves and include the Blue Whale, the world's largest mammal. It can weigh 160 tons and reach 30m in length. The largest of the toothed whales is the Sperm Whale, which can reach 18m in length. The toothed whales are composed of six families, including the Physeteridae (Sperm Whale), Delphinidae (dolphins), Phocoenidae (true porpoises) and Ziphiidae (beaked whales).

Whales need to come to the surface for air to avoid drowning. They have evolved extraordinary adaptations to help them dive to great depths without suffering from nitrogen narcosis, or 'the bends'. Beaked whales can hold their breath for two hours on long dives, and Sperm Whales have been recorded diving to depths of more than 2km.

The species accounts for the marine mammals are compact and focussed on identification. Most of the species covered in this book will be found close to the continental shelf. However, beaked whales occupy a different habitat, frequenting submarine canyons, so are almost never seen on commercial whale-watching trips, which go to the continental shelf. A few species such as Orcas hunt large marine mammals. Details of surface behaviour are described in more detail in *Wild Sri Lanka* (p. 170).

In Sri Lanka, at the time of writing, there is a high incidence of cetaceans, including Blue Whales, being killed in collisions with commercial ships. In an article I wrote in 2019, I also drew attention to fishermen being killed in collisions, and suggested the campaign to move the shipping lanes further south by 15 nautical miles be based on the need to improve safety for fishermen and shipping. Moving the shipping lanes for this reason will help to gain support and also reduce ship strikes on whales.

BALAENOPTERIDAE (BALEEN WHALES)

The baleen whales are so named because they have sheets of baleen in their mouths that they use to filter prey, which they catch by engulfing vast amounts of water containing fish or krill. The family includes the Blue Whale, the largest animal to have ever lived on the planet. At least eight species are recognized, all in the genus *Balaenoptera* except for the Humpback Whale in the genus *Megaptera*. They all have two blowholes that are set above the eyes on a long snout, or dorsum.

Blue Whale ◾ *Balaenoptera musculus indica*

Skin appears smooth but on close views shows mottling on blue-grey background. Dorsal fin set back about two-thirds and tiny, at times like a little hook. Blow tall and vertical, and can be three storeys high. Dorsal fin emerges after rostrum and blow are seen.

SUBSPECIES & DISTRIBUTION Subspecies of the Blue Whale found off Sri Lankan waters shorter than that found in higher latitudes (Atlantic, North Pacific and Antarctic), Antarctic length can be as much as 33m. Total length of northern Indian Ocean subspecies more than 10m shorter, about 20m. Shorter tail stock a feature that is apparent in the field and when reviewing images. Tail stock more elongated in larger subspecies. Four subspecies recognized by several authors, with unnamed subspecies from Chile also recognized by a few authors. *Indica* found in Northern Indian Ocean in seas from Bay of Bengal to Arabian Peninsula; *musculus* across Northern Pacific and Northern Atlantic; *intermedia* in high southern latitudes near Antarctica. *Musculus* and *intermedia* have latitudinal movements to feeding areas between winter and summer. Names commonly applied to subspecies as follows: Northern Blue Whale *B. m. musculus*, North Atlantic and North Pacific populations; Indian Ocean Blue Whale *B. m. indica*, Northern Indian Ocean; Pygmy Blue Whale *B. m. brevicauda*, subantarctic zone in mid to high latitudes in southern hemisphere; Southern Blue Whale *B. m. intermedia*, high southern latitudes summering in the Antarctic. **BEHAVIOUR** Usually seen singly or as mother and calf pair. Presence of calves suggests that it may be using Bay of Bengal as calving area. Songs of Blue Whales can be detected across a few thousand kilometres, so may be in contact with other individuals despite not being in close physical proximity. When feeding, they surface every 10–12 minutes and spend a few minutes at the surface. **DIET** Krill and mysids, fed on by gulp feeding. Typically feeds in top 60m.

Notched tail

Tall, vertical blow

Bryde's Whale ▪ *Balaenoptera edeni*

Three ridges on rostrum diagnostic. However, they are almost impossible to see from whale-watching boats used in Sri Lanka, and view from high vantage is needed. Sickle-shaped dorsal fin an easier field character. Most whale-watching crews now have their eye in and

Continued on p. 134.

Three diagnostic rostrum ridges

Sickle-shaped dorsal fin

are quick to identify a Bryde's when they see one. Much smaller than the Blue Whale (p. 132) and more uniformly coloured, but at sea, size, colouration and colour patterns hard to distinguish. Because size is not easy to compare, in Sri Lankan waters Bryde's may be mistaken for Blue, if dorsal fin is not seen. Bryde's may also surface so that head and dorsal fin emerge together, but this is not consistent and not reliable as an identification feature. **DISTRIBUTION** Largely confined to warm tropical waters, occasionally straying to higher latitudes. **BEHAVIOUR** In Sri Lanka generally solitary, but elsewhere can form loose groups of anything from half a dozen close to each other, to 10–30 spread over a few kilometres. **DIET** Varies from plankton to small fish; feeds by gulp feeding. Similar Species: Omura's Whale *B. omurai* has been photographed from Mirissa. This was once considered conspecific with Bryde's. Omura's has single rostral ridge (not three) and asymmetrical pigmentation on throat. Whitish throat and jaw on right side and dark on left side – characteristics that are not easy to observe from whale-watching boats. Omura's considered to be typically found in west Pacific in Southeast Asia. Some authors distinguish between a larger form Bryde's, *B. brydei*, found in western north Pacific Ocean and eastern Indian Ocean, and a small-form Bryde's that they prefer to call Eden's Whale *B. edeni*, found in Hong Kong, Australia and south-western Japan. There have been reliable sight records of small Eden's-type whales from the south since commercial whale watching took off after May 2008. These small whales may have been confused in the past with minke whales, raising the possibility that both forms or what are possibly two different species occur in Sri Lankan waters.

Fin Whale ■ *Balaenoptera physalus*

Although there are records in the literature, the absence of recent records from Sri Lanka and any records from the Maldives raises the possibility of mistaken identification with early records, when information on identification was less advanced and less readily available. However, it cannot be ruled out that Fin Whale visits Sri Lankan waters; it is included here (but not in the checklist) to assist observers. Asymmetrical patterning on jaws. Right-hand side has white lower jaw and white chevron above upper jaw covering right-hand side of face. Left-hand side dark. Backwards-facing, concave dorsal fin variable but more well defined, and relatively larger than dorsal on the Blue Whale (p. 132). Good views/photographs of right-side jaw and dorsal help in identification. Fin also uniformly dark and lacks mottling on Blue, but good lighting conditions are necessary to see this. Viewed under water, Fin had 'flipper shadows' or long, dark, rounded patches on sides where dark upperside meets white underside near pectoral flippers. Possible confusion species are Blue Whales of similar size, Bryde's Whale (p. 133), which also has prominent dorsal fin, and Omura's Whale *B. omurai*, which shares asymmetrical patterning with Fin. **DISTRIBUTION** High latitude and temperate waters, occurs in tropics. **BEHAVIOUR** Long-lived (85 years plus), and generally solitary or in pairs. **DIET** Krill and other crustaceans.

Asymmetrical jaw pattern

Dorsal fin larger than on Blue Whale

Northern Minke Whale ▪ *Balaenoptera acutorostrata*

Smallest rorqual. Flippers important for field identification but often not seen. White mid-band that contrasts strongly with dark upper surface, although degree of contrast can be quite weak in some geographical subspecies. The Dwarf Minke (a potentially new *Balaenoptera* species) has white upper flippers with dark trailing edge tipped black. In the

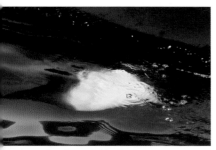

Antarctic Minke *B. bonaerensis*, upper surface of flippers mainly greyish. All three have dark upperparts and dorsal fin that is prominently sickle shaped and placed about two-thirds of the way back. All are small and streamlined. Snout (rostrum) triangular and pointed with single dorsal ridge. All three have chevron or blaze behind pectoral flipper that extends from pale underside to dark upperside. Curves forwards in Northern and Dwarf; tapers to point in Dwarf. **BEHAVIOUR** Usually solitary or in twos and threes. In high-latitude feeding grounds, large concentrations of a few hundred may gather and spread across several square kilometres. Easily overlooked, with weak, vertical, bushy blow. **DIET** Krill and small schooling fish taken by gulp feeding. **SIMILAR SPECIES** Based on geographical distributions, it is assumed that Minke recorded in Sri Lanka is the Northern rather than Dwarf or Antarctic. Some authors do not accept that minke whales have occurred in Sri Lankan waters. It is possible that Eden's Whale (see Bryde's Whale, p. 133), a smaller type of Bryde's Whale (or a full species), may have been confused with minke whales.

White flipper mid-band

Sickle-shaped dorsal fin and chevron (blaze) on side

Humpback Whale ▪ *Megaptera novaeangliae*

One of the most familiar whales due to extensive images of breaching Humpbacks photographed typically in North America. Long pectoral fins with extensive white on one side and large protuberances on edges not found in any other whale, but may not be visible. Tail distinctive, with ragged trailing edges and points at tip; underside has much white. Upper surface of head has central ridge and large protuberances. Many claims of Humpback sightings are from people who have seen Sperm Whales (p. 139) arching their backs before a dive and guessing they are 'humpbacks'. Unfortunately, I have made my own contribution to mistaken records by mistaking what may have been Blue Whales (p. 132) breaching at a distance in a courtship chase for Humpbacks. A skilled observer with close views of a Humpback is likely to see key identification characteristics. Blow of Humpback similar to that of Blue, and it may not be easy to distinguish a Humpback from a Blue from their blows alone in Sri Lanka. Dorsal fin small, stubby and quite variable in shape, and not reliable characteritic for telling the species apart. Tail stock has 'knuckles', or ridges',

which are not conspicuous as in Sperm Whales. Blues lack these 'knuckles' and have smooth tail stock. Humpbacks darker

Continued on p. 138.

Long pectoral flippers

Vertical blow

Protuberances on rostrum

Ragged trailing edge and pointed ends on tail

on upperside than Blues, but this is not a reliable characteristic as lighting conditions can render Blues a similar shade and pattern. **DISTRIBUTION** Individuals seen off Sri Lanka may belong to an Arabian Sea population, although this had not yet been confirmed through photo identification. Despite many claims, a critical review of records between December 2008 and December 2018 concluded that there were no more than six reliable records supported by photographs. **BEHAVIOUR** Social animals, typically encountered in groups that may be loosely spread or working together to catch fish. Records in Sri Lanka are of solitary individuals, or mother and calf pairs. **DIET** Uses baleen plates to filter water for small marine animals, but also known to catch fish, especially using 'bubble-netting' technique.

Mother and calf

Tail underside highly variable

> **PHYSETERIDAE (SPERM WHALE)**
> The Sperm Whale, the largest toothed carnivore in the world, is the only species in its family, although Dwarf and Pygmy Sperm Whales were previously included in the family. Morphologically the Sperm Whale is different from all other cetaceans, being adapted to diving very deep, down to 3km, and possessing a spermaceti organ in the head that is the world's largest natural sonar. It also has the largest brain of any animal.

Sperm Whale ■ *Physeter macrocephalus*

Largest toothed carnivore in the world, with male weighing to 55 metric tonnes and female 20 metric tonnes. Pronounced sexual dimorphism. Fairly easy to identify, with box-shaped snout, small, conical dorsal fin and grey, wrinkled body. Tail stock has 'knuckles'. Tail fin triangular with notch in middle. Does not extend out on flat edge like classic whale tails of Blue and Humpback Whales (pp. 132 and 137). Blow short and bushy, and points forwards and to one side. By contrast, blow of Blue rises in vertical column. When I first began watching whales in April 2008 from south of Mirissa, one of the first whales I saw was a Sperm Whale, which the boat crew claimed was a Blue; this indicates how little was known then of Sri Lanka's potential for whale watching. It is unlikely that any seasoned whale-watching crew will now make such a mistake.

Adult female tail slapping

Most likely to be encountered in February–mid-April, after Blue and Bryde's Whales. Its appearance, however, is erratic – it may occur in super-pods of more than 100, and Sri Lanka is the best place in the world to see a Sperm Whale super-pod; in fact, super-pods of the size seen in Sri Lanka are not seen anywhere else. Anyone interested in learning more should read my articles about this. In some older

Continued on p. 140.

Blow forward and to left

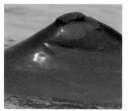

Calluses

Single blowhole

Wrinkly skin

whale-watching books there are claims that they gather in the thousands, but as I have clarified in one of my published articles, these have arisen from a misinterpretation of the technical literature. In most parts of the world, seeing more than 10 together is unusual. **DISTRIBUTION** One of the most widely distributed animals in the world, occurring in all oceans except on Arctic and Antarctic ice shelves. **BEHAVIOUR** Most pods in tropical latitudes comprise female and young, with adult bulls preferring higher latitudes and joining breeding schools to mate. Females have calluses on dorsal fins that are a secondary sexual characteristic. Scarring on bodies of mature bulls gained in fights with rival males. **DIET** Marked preference for squid, many of which live at depths of 400m. This explains why Sperm Whale pods patrol along a north–south axis near Kalpitiya Peninsula, where the continental shelf suddenly plunges to these depths.

Scarred mature bull

Logging (resting) whales

Kogiidae (Dwarf & Pygmy Sperm Whales)

This family is most closely related to the Physeteroidea (Sperm Whale) family. It contains just two species in the genus *Kogia*. Both have a shark-like appearance with a pointed snout in profile. They have overlapping ranges in warm and temperate waters. The jaws are underslung with a blunt, squarish head, characteristics shared with the Sperm Whale. Both have a crescent or gill-like mark behind and below the eye. This could be a form of visual mimicry of a shark to avoid being predated. The blowhole is located above the eye, slightly left of centre. By contrast, in the Sperm Whale the blowhole is positioned well in front (and to the left). The rostrum (part of the head in front of the eyes) is the shortest found in cetaceans. The left nostril, used for breathing, is seven times larger than the right one, used in the production of sound. Together with the Sperm Whale, these are the only cetaceans to possess a spermaceti organ. Both species tend to sink vertically into the water rather than engaging in a roll and exposing the tail stock before a dive.

Dwarf Sperm Whale ▪ *Kogia sima*

Very similar in size and appearance to the Pygmy Sperm Whale *K. breviceps*. Adult Dwarf 2.5m long versus 3m in Pygmy. Face of both species has shark-like appearance. Snout more pointed in Dwarf; rounded in Pygmy. Falcate dorsal fin highly variable and can have

Continued on p. 142.

pointed tip or be rounded. Dwarf's dorsal consistently erect, whereas in Pygmy it leans backwards. In Dwarf, head to mid-back curve of body fairly even or flat. Pygmy has hint of hump. Upperparts dark and underparts whitish. **DISTRIBUTION** Tropical to temperate waters. Prefers shallow waters close to continental shelf. **BEHAVIOUR** Usually solitary or in small groups of to 10. Not active on the surface and easily missed. **DIET** Cephalopods and fish.

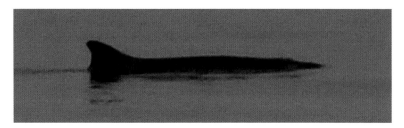

Pygmy Sperm Whale ■ *Kogia breviceps*

Very similar in size and appearance to the Dwarf Sperm Whale (see p.141). Distinct hump

Rounded, hooked dorsal fin

on back of head (almost vertically above eye), but note Dwarf also has this feature. Head not visible on surface. Dorsal fin tiny, rounded and hooked, different from Dwarf. Wrinkly skin but hard to see. Pale, circular mark (supercilium) above eye. Short, broad flipper set well forward. **DISTRIBUTION** Tropical and temperate seas, favours coastal and continental shelf zone. **BEHAVIOUR** Undemonstrative. May dive to 300m. Solitary or in groups up to 10. **DIET** Cephalopods, fish and crustaceans.

Mother and calf

> ### ZIPHIIDA (BEAKED WHALES)
> Beaked whales are among the least known whales because of their deep diving habits and inconspicuous behaviour at the surface. Their surface roll typically involves the beak emerging first at a steep angle. They have small flippers and a small, triangular dorsal fin set well back. The tail fluke is typically without a notch or only barely notched. Males use tusks for fighting. These 'erupt' and are exposed and colonized by barnacles. Many beaked whales have been described to science from strandings as they are so difficult to study out at sea.

Cuvier's Beaked Whale ▪ *Ziphius cavirostris*

Recognized by pale head that contrasts with body. Sloping forehead (that is, no pronounced melon) and short beak. Head somewhat concave in profile. Shape and colour of head distinguish it from other beaked whales. Body colour dark grey to reddish-brown. Rotund body. Mature males have two small teeth that have erupted from lower jaw. They also have linear scars from fights with other males.

DISTRIBUTION Tropical to northern latitudes, except in very high latitudes.

BEHAVIOUR Seen alone or in small groups of 2–3. Most often seen beaked whale in the world, but no recent records in Sri Lanka. It may be that they are not being looked for over submarine canyons.

DIET Beaked whales feed on squid and fish that live deep down. Known to frequent submarine canyons and dive deep for feeding.

Heavy scarring on a male

Deraniyagala's Beaked Whale ▪ *Mesoplodon hotaula*

First described to science by P. E. P. Deraniyagala in 1963. Two years later thought to be a synonym for rare Ginkgo-toothed Beaked Whale M. *ginkgodens*, and lost in synonymy until, on the basis of new morphometric and genetic evidence, it was restored as a new species in a 2014 paper. Cranium and mandible measurements used in paper were based on museum specimens. Images in this book are of a group photographed in the Maldives by Dr Charles Anderson, an author of the 2014 paper. Field identification characteristics require more observations. Based on recently dead specimens, colour described as blue-grey ventrally with blue-black on upperparts extending to form dark cap on head, which is slender with an elongate beak. Eye half beak length behind gape. Body compressed. Area around eye mottled grey becoming lighter lower down, contrasting with white of throat, and lower jaw predominantly white with grey tip. Gingko-toothed specimens from New Zealand described as brownish-grey on upperparts, but Japanese animals described as having blue-black upperparts. Therefore, colour alone cannot be used to separate the two species. **DISTRIBUTION** First individual washed ashore in Ratmalana, a little south of Colombo. Specimens in museums also collected from islands in Palmyra Atoll about 1,770 km from Hawaii, Seychelles and Gilbert Islands, Republic of Kiribati. **BEHAVIOUR** Very little known. Gilbert islanders claimed it is driven ashore a few times a year in hunts by islanders. This is unusual, as beaked whales are creatures of deep canyons and only come to shallow waters during strandings. **DIET** Unknown but probably marine vertebrates that live in deep water.

Very few photographs have been taken of live Deraniyagala's Beaked Whales in the wild. This distant image is one of a few available at the time of going to press

Blainville's Beaked Whale ▪ *Mesoplodon densirostris*

The sole Sri Lankan record is based on one photographed in a fish market by Lester Perera. One of Sri Lanka's foremost marine biologists, Anouk Ilangakoon, subsequently identified it. Forehead flat with an indistinct melon. Colour varies from warm brown above to dark grey. Small dorsal fin triangular with wide base, set about two-thirds of the way back. Lower jaw strongly arched with teeth erupting at the top of the arch in males. Adults reach a length of 6m. **DISTRIBUTION** Recorded worldwide in tropical and temperate oceans. **BEHAVIOUR** Found in small groups. May emerge beak first. Blow is indistinct. May slap beak on water's surface. Adult males may show heavy scarring from fights. **DIET** Squid and fish.

Triangular dorsal fin with wide base

Strongly arched lower jaw

Longman's Beaked Whale ■ *Indopacetus pacificus*

(Tropical Bottlenose Whale)

Can be confused with Cuvier's Beaked Whale (p. 143), but forehead more pronounced and has prominent beak. The only whale in Indian Ocean and tropical Pacific with bottlenose. Robust, with prominent and falcate dorsal fin, set well back. Melon well developed and in

mature males can have an overhang. Head pale and line of demarcation with darker upper body behind blowhole. Dark band from eye to pectoral flipper, bordering high, pale thoracic panel. Blow bushy and forwards facing. Fast swimmer that shows entire head when swimming fast. **DISTRIBUTION** Fairly restricted range in Indian Ocean and tropical Pacific. **BEHAVIOUR** Gregarious; found in small pods of 15–20, although pods of 100 recorded. Males have linear scars resulting from fighting with other males. **DIET** Unknown, but probably marine vertebrates that live in deep water.

Pronounced forehead and 'bottlenose' beak

Falcate dorsal fin

DELPHINIDAE (OCEAN DOLPHINS)

This family with 36 species in 17 genera accounts for 40 per cent of all cetacean species, and has a worldwide distribution. Ocean dolphins vary greatly in size from small to medium, with dorsal fins of varying size. They have pointed, conical teeth. The tail flukes have a median notch. Like other toothed cetaceans they have a single blowhole. Despite advances in molecular phylogenetics, resolving the relationships of the various ocean dolphins remains problematic and various subfamilies have been proposed within the family. It is likely that superficially similar species may be reassigned to different genera; their similarities are likely to have arisen from convergence rather than from them being sister species. Molecular evidence also suggests that populations in different parts of the world of what is considered to be a single species may be more than one species. The split of Indo-Pacific and Common Bottlenose Dolphins is a case in point. Interestingly, it appears that the Indo-Pacific Bottlenose Dolphin may be more closely related to species currently placed in other genera (*Stenella* and *Delphinus*) than to the Common Bottlenose Dolphin.

Killer Whale ▪ *Orcinus orca*

(Orca)

Very distinctively marked oceanic dolphin that can prey on whales, hence the name Killer Whale. Probably one of the best known and iconic cetaceans, and one of the most widespread, often with local populations that appear to have their own repertoire of vocalizations, colour patterns and behaviour. In north-east Pacific, where it has been studied for many years, three ecotypes recognized: resident or coastal fish eaters, mammal eaters or transients, and offshore, large-school types. Four types also recognized in Antarctic. **BEHAVIOUR** Mammal-eating forms occur in smaller groups of 5–10, fish-eating forms in larger groups of 20–200. Pods encountered in Sri Lanka probably mammal-eating transients that travel widely. Many years ago I suggested to Georgina Gemmell that she maintain a record of sightings together with a photo identification catalogue of Orcas from Sri Lanka. This grew into the

Continued on p. 148.

Paddle-shaped pectorals

Males have tall, erect dorsal fins

Orca Project Sri Lanka (OPSL) administered by her and OPSL, which has recorded more than 39 individuals since 2007. Two Orcas are often sighted together and have also been seen off United Arab Emirates in Arabian Sea. Sri Lanka does not have resident pods and appearance of Orcas is sporadic. With an improved network of reporting, records come in every year to OPSL. Adult males told apart from females and juveniles by tall dorsal fin. All Orcas have white eye-patch and pale saddle behind dorsal fin. Some discrete populations share common pattern. Social animals, often seen in small pods, although in Sri Lanka, two individuals often seen together just as a pair. **DIET** Fish or small mammals, depending on which ecotype they are. In Sri Lanka, Orcas have been filmed attacking Sperm Whales (p. 139).

Orcas recorded in Sri Lanka are typically in small pods

False Killer Whale ■ *Pseudorca crassidens*

All-dark dolphin, beakless with blunt head. Best identification feature if seen is kinked pectoral flippers. Furthermore, a cape is barely discernible and shows no dip near dorsal fin. Lacks white lips. These three features help separate it from similar Pygmy Killer Whale and Melon-headed Whale (pp. 150 and 151). Shape of dorsal fin also differs in False Killer by having more narrow base with tip more rounded. Melon does not slope down as in Melon-headed and head more rounded. **DISTRIBUTION** Tropical and subtropical waters with range extending to nearly temperate waters. **BEHAVIOUR** Fast-moving and active dolphin that bow rides. Found in pods of 10–100. Often associates with other dolphin species. **DIET** Fish and cephalopods. Also preys on other, smaller dolphins and even whales.

No white lips

Kinked pectoral fins

Tip of dorsal fin rounded

Pygmy Killer Whale ▪ *Feresa attenuata*

Rather dark, small dolphin with small, irregular area of white on underside (white ventral area unlikely to be seen by whale watchers). Key features to look for are white lips on dark, almost black head and melon curving gently to mouth line to create rounded head with no beak. Some individuals have more extensive white patches around lips. Dorsal fin erect and swept backwards with trailing edge sickle shaped. Narrow, dark cape extends from head to tail stock, tapering to point behind dorsal fin. Cape not obvious as it is dark

against dark. Pectoral fins round tipped; may show when moving fast. Shares many features with similar Melon-headed Whale (opposite). Latter has sloping melon – the best distinguishing feature. In Melon-headed pectorals pointed rather than rounded at tip – a subtle difference. **DISTRIBUTION** Worldwide in tropical and subtropical waters. Rarely seen in Sri Lankan waters. Generally shy of boats. **BEHAVIOUR** Found in small schools of to 25. **DIET** Cephalopods and fish. Believed to prey on other dolphin species.

Erect dorsal fin, falcate on trailing edge

Melon-headed Whale ■ *Peponocephala electra*

Similar to Pygmy Killer Whale (opposite), sharing overall dark colour with narrower darker cape and white lips. Key distinguishing features are melon sloping down to lips and pectoral flippers pointed rather than rounded at tip. Head shape therefore conical rather than blunt. Dorsal fin tall and falcate as in Pygmy Killer. In Melon-headed, cape makes pronounced dip as it flows past dorsal fin. In Pygmy Killer dip not so pronounced. The False Killer Whale's (p. 149) cape is barely discernible and does not make pronounced dip as it sweeps past dorsal fin. False Killer also has kinked pectorals that do not form graceful curve. **DISTRIBUTION** Tropical and subtropical waters in large pods of 100–500. **BEHAVIOUR** Fast swimming and boisterous. Can be found rafting. Rare in Sri Lankan waters. **DIET** Fish, squid and crustaceans.

Erect, falcate dorsal fin

Head shape conical, not blunt (not visible in picture)

Short-finned Pilot Whale ■ *Globicephala macrorhynchus*

Very dark, looking black at times. Chunky bodied with bulbous head, bigger that of Spinner Dolphin (p. 160). Dorsal fin has broad base and curves back. In older males, fin

very large and blunt, almost flag shaped. **DISTRIBUTION** The Long-finned Pilot Whale G. *melas* (not recorded from Sri Lanka) occurs in northern hemisphere in temperate to subarctic Atlantic waters. In southern hemisphere found in high latitudes close to ice-free Antarctic waters. Its disjunct distribution overlaps in some places with distribution of Short-finned, found from about 40 degrees south to 50 degrees north in latitude. **BEHAVIOUR** In small pods when seen off Sri Lanka, but elsewhere can occur in pods of several hundred. Often seen in company of bottlenose dolphins. **DIET** Fish, squid and octopus.

Broad-based fin

Bulbous head and enormous fin in adult

Risso's Dolphin
■ *Grampus griseus*

Identified by bulbous, square-shaped head. Dorsal fin high and curved back (falcate). Upperparts vary from dark to pale. Older dolphins paler and very heavily scarred. Well known for heavy scarring on body. Juveniles darker, lack scarring and may be confused with other, smaller 'blackfish' species such as Pygmy Killer, Melon-headed and False Killer Whales (pp. 150, 151 and 149). However, adults usually present with juveniles and help to eliminate confusion. **DISTRIBUTION** Tropical and temperate waters. Scarce in Sri Lanka, with encounter rates as low as 3 per cent based on data on over 1,000 whale-watching sailings. Flippers pointed; feature not always visible. **BEHAVIOUR** Typically in pods varying from a few individuals to about 50. In Sri Lanka, sightings often of small pods containing less than 12. Appearances associated with presence of other dolphins. Speed of travel slower than that of Spinner Dolphin (p. 160). **DIET** Feeds mainly at night on squid, cuttlefish, octopus and krill.

Squarish head

Very heavily scarred male

High, curved back dorsal fin

Rough-toothed Dolphin ■ *Steno bredanensis*

Characteristic reptilian face created by gently sloping forehead and beak. Falcate dorsal fin broad based and relatively tall and erect. Pointed in young animals and more rounded in older individuals. White lips on upper jaw, and white lower jaw and underparts. Dark cape offers little contrast and hard to make out. Flippers relatively large but not easy to see.

Generally unlikely to be confused with any other species. **DISTRIBUTION** Tropical and subtropical oceans. Very rarely seen in Sri Lankan waters, perhaps because it favours deep water and most whale watching takes place at shallower depths near continental shelf, or may be naturally scarce in northern Indian Ocean. **BEHAVIOUR** Often in company of other dolphin species. Small groups of 5–10, although groups of a few hundred have been recorded elsewhere. Sluggish swimmer that does not porpoise out of the water. **DIET** Mainly cephaloapods and fish.

Broad-based fin

Reptilian face

Indo-Pacific Humpback Dolphin ■ *Sousa chinensis*

Grey and pink with distinctive wide base to dorsal fin, giving rise to 'hump-back'. Mature adults show a lot of pink, especially on tail and belly. Requires focused search in Puttalam Lagoon, usually accessed from Kalpitiya Peninsula, with encounter rate of about one in three trips. Seems very rare and recent records only from Kalpitiya. Those seen around Sri Lanka are 'Plumbaea' type, with more grey and less pink than those further east in Asia. **DISTRIBUTION** Inshore species found from southern tip of Africa, across Middle East, to east Asia towards Japan. From east Asia occurs all the way south across Indonesian archipelago, New Guinea and northern Australia. **BEHAVIOUR** In Sri Lanka, I have only seen it in small pods of 5–10, but in some parts of range there are records of about 1,000 forming pods. Sometimes seen in mixed pods with Common Bottlenose Dolphins (p. 156). **DIET** Cephalopods and fish hunted in shallow waters around reefs and estuaries.

Broad base to dorsal fin

Broad tail-fin with straight trailing edge on

Blunt 'bottlenose'

Common Bottlenose Dolphin ■ *Tursiops truncatus*

Uniformly grey with blunt tip – the 'bottle-nose'. I have seen it infrequently, close to Mirissa Harbour. Probably overlooked as much less acrobatic than 'spinners'. Split into two species with the Indo-Pacific Bottlenose Dolphin (opposite). Latter characterized by spotting in ventral area, and has more slender proportions, less convex melon, proportionately taller dorsal fin and more slender beak. Ranges of the two species overlap and they can be found in mixed pods. In Sri Lanka, bottlenose dolphins seen close to shore are generally Indo-Pacific, which has longer, slimmer beak. **DISTRIBUTION** Worldwide from tropics to temperate oceans. **BEHAVIOUR** Considered more 'playful' than Indo-Pacific. It is hard for all but the most experienced observers to tell the two species apart in field conditions. However, they have strong genetic and other morphological differences such as in the teeth. Some individuals have contrasting cape. **DIET** Fish, squid, crustaceans and krill.

Unspotted underparts

Indo-Pacific Bottlenose Dolphin ▪ *Tursiops aduncus*

Looks very similar to the Common Bottlenose Dolphin (opposite). Slightly smaller and slimmer but this is not readily apparent in the field. Centrally placed dorsal fin proportionately taller and broad based. Ventral area can have variable amount of spotting, absent in some individuals. Spotting may not be visible from a boat unless an individual breaches out of the water. Indo-Pacific has longer, slimmer beak. **DISTRIBUTION** Inshore waters from eastern coastline of Africa, across Middle East, south Asia and Southeast Asia, to Pacific in east Asia, and northern Australia and New Guinea. **BEHAVIOUR** More subdued than in Common Bottlenose. **DIET** Fish and cephalopods, hunting near reefs. Captures prey from sea bed.

More slender 'bottlenose' beak and proportionally taller dorsal fin than in the Common Bottlenose Dolphin

Long-beaked Common Dolphin ■ *Delphinus capensis*

Long-beaked and Short-beaked Common Dolphins *D. delphis* were split in 1994 – genus may actually contain more than two species. Subtle differences between the two: Short-beaked has rounder head, stockier beak and cleaner, yellow thoracic panel. Facial area around eye cleaner. Subspecies of Long-beaked found in Sri Lanka, *D. c. tropicalis*, has distinctly longer beak. **DISTRIBUTION** Coastal waters around Africa, Middle East, and south and Southeast Asia to east Asia, west coast of North America, and west and east coasts of South America. Range of Short-beaked can overlap but it is found across Pacific and Atlantic Oceans; very rare in Sri Lanka. **BEHAVIOUR** Always in small pods of 10–30 but can coalesce into aggregations of a few hundred. In Sri Lanka likely to be seen in small pods. **DIET** Fish, squid and krill.

Distinctly long beak and obvious thoracic panel

Fraser's Dolphin ■ *Lagenodelphis hosei*

Short-beaked with broad black band from beak and across eye to anal keel. Thinner stripe from eye to relatively short flippers. Thick black band across eye like a 'highwayman's mask', extending across forehead, but thinner. Dorsal fin erect, triangular and at times falcate. Little contrast between dark cape and dark grey sides. Black lateral band bordered on top by thin pale band. Underparts pale, at times with pink flush. May be confused with the Striped Dolphin (p. 162), which has much thinner stripes. Striped has indistinct grey blaze and additional thin, short black stripe behind eye.
DISTRIBUTION Warm oceans worldwide, in latitudinal band that roughly spans Africa from north to south.
BEHAVIOUR Found in tight-knit pods.
DIET Cephalopods, crustaceans and fish.

Black band from beak, across eye to anal keel

Short beak

Spinner Dolphin ■ *Stenella longirostris*

Most frequently encountered cetacean in Sri Lankan waters. Easily identified by thin, long snout and elongated head. Different populations around the world with a range of patterns. Some uniformly dark above, whereas those found off Sri Lanka have three-toned appearance with stripey look. More taxonomic work and study of vocalization may result in splits. 'Spinners' off Sri Lanka have nearly triangular dorsal fins with small backwards curve. Eye to flipper and eye to anus stripes fairly simple and not complex as in Striped, Fraser's or Long-beaked Common Dolphins (pp. 162, 159 and 158). **DISTRIBUTION** Dolphin of warm waters with worldwide range, extending to subtropics. **BEHAVIOUR** It is not uncommon to see pods with more than 500 individuals. On one occasion I

encountered one of the well-known super-pods in Kalpitiya that stretched across 1km and had over 2,000 individuals. However, most accounts of pods containing thousands are probably exaggerated. In a large pod, many individuals spin. A reason for doing this is that it dislodges remoras, parasitic fish that attach themselves to a dolphin's body. Spinning may occur for other reasons, including courtship, establishing a pecking order, demonstrating fitness or just having fun. **DIET** Varied, from marine invertebrates to small fish. Fish the main component of diet, and local fishermen use presence of pods to alert them to shoaling fish.

Forehead crease

Three-toned, stripey look, and long, thin beak

Pantropical Spotted Dolphin ■ *Stenella attenuata*

Tip of beak has pale spot. Dark cape on top of light body, and on the surface looks two-toned like a Spinner Dolphin (opposite). Check for absence of eye to anal stripe. Also lacks eye to flipper stripe, and instead has lower jaw to flipper stripe. Shape of pale area gives it an obvious 'pale face' compared to Spinner's. Those seen around Sri Lanka are of offshore variety that has hardly any spots on top. **DISTRIBUTION** Worldwide in tropical waters. **BEHAVIOUR** Highly social. Likes to bow ride. Occasionally leaps out of the water. Pods of 10–20 seen in Sri Lanka. Elsewhere, pods numbering 1,000 recorded. Lives to 46 years. **DIET** Cephalopods, crustaceans and fish.

Pale tip to beak

No eye-to-flipper and eye-to-anus stripes

Striped Dolphin ■ *Stenella coeruleoalba*

Two clear stripes from eye to flipper and anus respectively. Both contrast strongly with pale sides. Eye to anus stripe has another short, thin line that breaks out near eye. Cape has paler blaze, variable in width, with a finger extending towards dorsal fin. Rest of

Stripe bifurcates

blaze extends along flanks above eye to anus black stripe. Short beaked with rounded melon. Triangular dorsal fin mildly falcate. Eye heavily bordered in black. Easily separated from the Pantropical Spotted Dolphin (p. 161), which does not have black eye to anus stripe and pale blaze. Pantropical also has narrow, pointed and falcate dorsal fin, very different in shape. Fraser's Dolphin (p. 159) is superficially similar to Striped, but eye to anus stripe is significantly fatter. Eye to anus and eye to flipper black lines, where they meet eye, very thick, and eye completely submerged in black. Fraser's lacks two-fingered pale blaze on cape, and its dorsal fin shape is also different by being erect, triangular and less backswept. **DISTRIBUTION** Tropical and temperate waters. **BEHAVIOUR** Fast-moving animal found in small pods. Can be acrobatic, often leaping high into the air. Does not associate often with other dolphins. **DIET** Fish and cephalopods.

Distinct sinuous eye-to-anus stripe

> **PHOCOENIDAE (PORPOISES)**
> Porpoises are relatively small marine mammals found in all oceans, with some occurring in rivers in east and south Asia. There are seven species in three genera. Ocean-dwelling porpoises generally prefer shallower waters inshore of the continental shelf. Two species are exceptions and prefer deep oceanic waters.

Indo-Pacific Finless Porpoise ■ *Neophocaena phocaenoides*

In 2011 what was a single species of Finless Porpoise was split into two species, the Indo-Pacific Finless Porpoise *N. phocaenoides* and Narrow-ridged Finless Porpoise *N. asiaorientalis*. Of the two species only the former is found in tropics and subtropics, the other preferring temperate latitudes. Indo-Pacific has smaller body length (171cm) than Narrow-ridged. Dorsal fin absent. Dorsal groove or ridge wider than in Narrow-ridged found in China and east Asia seas. Head blunt with no beak, and with broad rostrum. General colouration dark grey to blackish. **DISTRIBUTION** From Persian Gulf to China and south to Sunda Islands, Indonesia. Coastal species and most records from Sri Lanka are from fishing bycatch or strandings. **BEHAVIOUR** Unobtrusive behaviour and low surface profile may contribute to it hardly ever being seen by whale-watching boats. Numbers may also have been depleted by coastal pollution and accidental entrapment in fishing nets. Chases fish at high speeds. **DIET** Fish, squid, cephalopods and crustaceans.

Blunt head with no beak, and no dorsal fin

· Checklist of the Mammals of Sri Lanka ·

Ninety-six terrestrial mammals are recognized in this checklist, although it is likely that the three golden palm civets are just one highly variable species. Twenty-nine cetaceans (whales and dolphins), two other marine mammals (the Dugong and a phocid seal) make a total of 31 marine mammals, resulting in a total of 127 species. The Fin Whale has not been included in the checklist as past records are likely to be misidentifications.

PROBOSCIDEA	
Elephantidae (Elephants)	
Asian Elephant	*Elephas maximus*
PRIMATES	
Lorisidae (Lorises)	
Red Slender Loris	*Loris tardigradus*
Grey Slender Loris	*Loris lydekkerianus*
Cercopithecidae (Old World Monkeys)	
Toque Macaque	*Macaca sinica*
Hanuman Langur	*Semnopithecus priam*
Purple-faced Leaf Monkey	*Semnopithecus vetulus*
RODENTIA	
Sciuridae (Squirrels)	
Layard's Palm Squirrel	*Funambulus layardi*
Indian Palm Squirrel	*Funambulus palmarum*
Sri Lanka Dusky-striped Squirrel	*Funambulus obscurus*
Giant Grey Flying Squirrel	*Petaurista philippensis*
Small Flying Squirrel	*Petinomys fuscocapillus*
Grizzled Indian Squirrel	*Ratufa macroura*
Cricetidae (Gerbils)	
Indian Gerbil	*Tatera indica*
Muridae (Rats & Mice)	
Lesser Bandicoot-Rat	*Bandicota bengalensis*
Greater Bandicoot-Rat	*Bandicota indica*
White-tailed Wood Rat	*Cremnomys blanfordi*
Indian Bush-Rat	*Golunda ellioti*
Eastern House Mouse	*Mus musculus*
Indian Field Mouse	*Mus booduga*
Sri Lanka Spiny Mouse	*Mus fernandoni*
Sri Lanka Bi-coloured Spiny Mouse	*Mus mayori*
Montane Rat	*Rattus montanus*
House Rat	*Rattus rattus*
Brown Rat	*Rattus norvegicus*
Ohiya Rat	*Srilankamys ohiensis*
Soft-furred Field Rat	*Millardia meltada*
Sri Lanka Highland Climbing Mouse	*Vandeleuria nolthenii*

Asiatic Long-tailed Climbing Mouse	*Vandeleuria oleracea*
Hystricidae (Porcupines)	
Indian Crested Porcupine	*Hystrix indica*
LAGOMORPHA	
Leporidae (Hares & Rabbits)	
Indian Hare	*Lepus nigricollis*
SORICOMORPHA	
Soricidae (Shrews)	
Horsfield's Shrew	*Crocidura horsfieldii*
Sri Lanka Long-tailed Shrew	*Crocidura miya*
Sinharaja Shrew	*Crocidura hikmiya*
Kelaart's Long-clawed Shrew	*Feroculus feroculus*
Pearson's Long-clawed Shrew	*Solisorex pearsoni*
House Shrew	*Suncus murinus*
Sri Lanka Shrew	*Suncus zeylanicus*
Pygmy Shrew	*Suncus etruscus*
Sri Lanka Pygmy Shrew	*Suncus fellowesgordoni*
Highland Shrew	*Suncus montanus*
CHIROPTERA	
Pteropodidae (Fruit Bats)	
Lesser Dog-faced Fruit Bat	*Cynopterus brachyotis*
Greater Short-nosed Fruit Bat	*Cynopterus sphinx*
Indian Flying Fox	*Pteropus medius*
Leschenault's Rousette	*Rousettus leschenaultii*
Megadermatidae (False Vampire Bats)	
Greater False Vampire	*Megaderma lyra*
Lesser False Vampire	*Megaderma spasma*
Rhinolophidae (Horseshoe Bats)	
Lesser Woolly Horseshoe Bat	*Rhinolophus beddomei*
Rufous Horseshoe Bat	*Rhinolophus rouxii*
Hipposideridae (Leaf-nosed or Round-leaf Bats)	
Dusky Leaf-nosed Bat	*Hipposideros ater*
Fulvous Leaf-nosed Bat	*Hipposideros fulvus*
Cantor's Leaf-nosed Bat	*Hipposideros galeritus*
Great Leaf-nosed Bat	*Hipposideros lankadiva*
Schneider's Leaf-nosed Bat	*Hipposideros speoris*
Emballonuridae (Sac-winged & Sheath-tailed Bats)	
Pouch-bearing Bat	*Saccolaimus saccolaimus*
Long-winged Tomb Bat	*Taphozous longimanus*
Black-bearded Tomb Bat	*Taphozous melanopogon*
Molossidae (Free-tailed Bats)	
Wrinkle-lipped Free-tailed Bat	*Chaerephon plicatus*
Egyptian Free-tailed Bat	*Tadarida aegyptiaca*
Vespertilionidae (Evening & Vesper Bats)	
Tickell's Bat	*Hesperoptenus tickelli*
Hardwicke's Wooly Bat	*Kerivoula hardwickii*

Painted Bat	*Kerivoula picta*
Round-eared Tube-nosed Bat	*Murina cyclotis*
Van Hasselt's Mouse-eared Bat	*Myotis hasseltii*
Horsfield's Mouse-eared Bat	*Myotis horsfieldii*
Kelaart's Pipistrelle	*Pipistrellus ceylonicus*
Indian Pipistrelle	*Pipistrellus coromandra*
Pygmy Pipistrelle	*Pipistrellus tenuis*
Chocolate Pipistrelle	*Falsistrellus affinis*
Asiatic Greater Yellow House Bat	*Scotophilus heathii*
Asiatic Lesser Yellow House Bat	*Scotophilus kuhlii*
Miniopteridae (Long-fingered Bats)	
Eastern Bent-winged Bat	*Miniopterous fuliginosus*
PHOLIDOTA	
Manidae (Pangolin)	
Indian Pangolin	*Manis crassicaudata*
CARNIVORA	
Felidae (Cats)	
Jungle Cat	*Felis chaus*
Rusty-spotted Cat	*Prionailurus rubiginosa*
Fishing Cat	*Prionailurus viverrina*
Leopard	*Panthera pardus kotiya*
Viverridae (Civets & Palm Civets)	
Common Palm Civet	*Paradoxurus hermaphroditus*
Wet-zone Golden Palm Civet	*Paradoxurus aureus*
Dry-zone Golden Palm Civet	*Paradoxurus stenocephalus*
Montane Golden Palm Civet	*Paradoxurus montanus*
Small Indian Civet	*Viverricula indica*
Herpestidae (Mongooses)	
Indian Grey Mongoose	*Herpestes edwardsii*
Indian Brown Mongoose	*Herpestes fuscus*
Ruddy Mongoose	*Herpestes smithii*
Stripe-necked Mongoose	*Herpestes vitticollis*
Canidae (Dogs)	
Golden Jackal	*Canis aureus*
Ursidae (Bears)	
Sloth Bear	*Melursus ursinus*
Mustelidae (Martens, Weasels, Badgers & Otters)	
Eurasian Otter	*Lutra lutra*
ARTIODACTYLA	
Suidae (Pigs)	
Wild Pig	*Sus scrofa*
Tragulidae (Chevrotains)	
White-spotted Mouse-deer	*Moschiola meminna*
Yellow-striped Mouse-deer	*Moschiola kathygre*
Cervidae (Deer)	
Spotted Deer	*Axis axis*

Hog Deer	*Axis porcinus*
Sambar	*Rusa unicolor*
Red Muntjac	*Muntiacus muntjak*
Bovidae (Hollow-horned Ruminants)	
Water Buffalo	*Bubalus bubalis*
SIRENIA	
Dugongidae (Dugong)	
Dugong	*Dugong dugon*
Phocidae (Earless Seals)	
Southern Elephant Seal	*Mirounga leonina*
CETACEA	
Balaenopteridae (Rorquals or Baleen Whales)	
Blue Whale	*Balaenoptera musculus indica*
Bryde's Whale	*Balaenoptera edeni*
Omura's Whale	*Balaenoptera omurai*
Northern Minke Whale	*Balaenoptera acutorostrata*
Humpback Whale	*Megaptera novaeangliae*
Physeteridae (Sperm Whale)	
Sperm Whale	*Physeter macrocephalus*
Kogiidae (Dwarf & Pygmy Sperm Whales)	
Pygmy Sperm Whale	*Kogia breviceps*
Dwarf Sperm Whale	*Kogia sima*
Ziphiidae (Beaked Whales)	
Cuvier's Beaked Whale	*Ziphius cavirostris*
Deraniyagala's Beaked Whale	*Mesoplodon hotaula*
Blainville's Beaked Whale	*Mesoplodon densirostris*
Longman's Beaked Whale	*Indopacetus pacificus*
Delphinidae (Ocean Dolphins)	
Killer Whale	*Orcinus orca*
False Killer Whale	*Pseudorca crassidens*
Pygmy Killer Whale	*Feresa attenuata*
Melon-headed Whale	*Peponocephala electra*
Short-finned Pilot Whale	*Globicephala macrorhynchus*
Risso's Dolphin	*Grampus griseus*
Rough-toothed Dolphin	*Steno bredanensis*
Indo-Pacific Humpback Dolphin	*Sousa chinensis*
Common Bottlenose Dolphin	*Tursiops truncatus*
Indo-Pacific Bottlenose Dolphin	*Tursiops aduncus*
Long-beaked Common Dolphin	*Delphinus capensis*
Fraser's Dolphin	*Lagenodelphis hosei*
Spinner Dolphin	*Stenella longirostris*
Pantropical Spotted Dolphin	*Stenella attenuata*
Striped Dolphin	*Stenella coeruleoalba*
Phocoenidae (Porpoises)	
Indo-Pacific Finless Porpoise	*Neophocaena phocaenoides*

FURTHER INFORMATION

INFORMATION FOR VISITORS

Some preparation can make a lot of difference in a small accessible island like Sri Lanka. A good deal of information is available both on the internet and in printed books.

Internet

Many internet sites offer past trip reports. A huge amount of information in the form of documents, presentations and PDFs can be copied using this link to the author's blog: https://wildlifewithgehan. blogspot.com/2016/01/sri-lanka-wildlife-publications.html. Some of the specialist wildlife tour operators' websites, such as www.jetwingeco.com, also contain a lot of information.

Books

For pre-trip reading, *Wild Sri Lanka* and *Sri Lankan Wildlife*, both authored by me, are useful. *Wild Sri Lanka* brings together key wildlife stories and highlights, and has a handy wildlife viewing calendar. Other field guides authored and photographed by me are available. Serious land-mammal enthusiasts should look out for two books, *Manual of the Mammals of Sri Lanka* and *The Mammals of Sri Lanka*. A wealth of detail on marine mammals can be found in *Whales and Dolphins of Sri Lanka* and *Out of the Blue*. For bat enthusiasts, *A Field Guide to the Bats of Sri Lanka* is useful. For a broader international perspective, nothing surpasses the nine-volume *The Handbook of the Mammals of the World* published by Lynx Edicions. For further details of these and other publications, see bibliography (p. 170).

Tour Operators

I mention Jetwing Eco Holidays, with whom I worked for many years, in the acknowledgements (p. 172). A non-exhaustive list is given below drawing mainly on companies that have supported my field work, together with a few others.

Adventure Birding www.adventurebirding.lk
Birding Sri Lanka www.birdingsrilanka.com
Bird and Wildlife Team www.birdandwildlifeteam.com
Eco Team (Mahoora Tented Safaris) www.srilankaecotourism.com
Jetwing Eco Holidays www.jetwingeco.com
Little Adventures www.littleadventuressrilanka.com
Natural World Explorer www.naturalworldexplorer.com
Nature Trails www.naturetrails.lk
Walk with Jith www.walkwithjith.com

WATCHING ANIMALS AT NIGHT

Night safaris for nocturnal animals can be a rewarding experience but should always be done with your personal safety and the welfare of the animals in mind. Do not go alone – always go with locals who know the trails. There are several dangers. Some trails have trap guns laid for illegally hunted animals. Elephants, bears and wild boars can kill or maim. In areas adjoining national parks and reserves spotlighting is not allowed, a legacy from legislation designed to curb poaching.

ORGANIZATIONS

Included here are what may appear to be bird- or plant-centric organizations, but their field meetings provide a good way to get out into good sites for mammals and meet people who know about them. Some of the organizations can also be found on social media.

NGOs
The Sri Lanka Natural History Society (SLNHS)
www.slnhs.lk, email: slnhs@lanka.ccom.lk.
Founded in 1912, and remains an active, albeit small society with core membership of enthusiasts and professionals in nature conservation. Organizes varied programme of talks, day trips, and longer excursions with one or more overnight stays.

Field Ornithology Group of Sri Lanka (FOGSL)
Department of Zoology, University of Colombo, Colombo 3. fogsl.cmb.ac.lk/, email: fogsl@cmb.ac.lk
Sri Lankan representative of BirdLife International. Has a programme of site visits and lectures throughout the year, and publishes *Malkoha* newsletter and other occasional publications.

Ruk Rakaganno, the Tree Society of Sri Lanka
http://rukrakaganno.wixsite.com/rukrakaganno, email: rukrakaganno09@gmail.com.
Works with communities, particularly women, to care for and protect water resources and biodiversity. Also concerned about trees in urban environment. Currently manages Popham-IFS Arboretum in Dambulla.

Wildlife and Nature Protection Society (WNPS)
86 Rajamalwatta Road, Battaramulla. www.wnpssl.org, email: wnps@sltnet.lk.
Publishes biannual journal, *Loris* (in English) and *Warana* (in Sinhala). Monthly lecture series are a sell-out success and if you need a seat you have to arrive early. Also organizes field trips.

The Young Zoologists' Association of Sri Lanka (YZA)
National Zoological Gardens, Dehiwala. www.yzasrilanka.lk, email: srilankayza@gmail.com, FacebookYoungZoologistsAssociationofSriLanka, Twitter: @yzasrilanka, YouTube: YZA Sri Lanka. Non-profit, non-governmental, voluntary youth organization based at National Zoological Gardens, Dehiwala. Meets at the Zoo every Sunday at 2 p.m.

State Institutions
Department of Wildlife Conservation of Sri Lanka (DWLC)
www.dwc.gov.lk.
Tasked with looking after fauna and administers national parks and many reserves.

Forest Department
www.forestdept.gov.lk/index.php/en.
Tasked with conservation and management of many of Sri Lanka's important forest reserves, including lowland rainforests. Has published small number of publications, and issues scientific journal *The Forester*.

International
Whale & Dolphin Conservation
https://uk.whales.org.
UK-based conservation charity active across the world. Has been involved in a number of training programmes in Sri Lanka to train local boat operators in responsible whale watching.

KEY SOURCES
W. W. A. Phillips's *Manual of the Mammals of Sri Lanka* remains an outstanding piece of work. It has

been a key source of reference for me ever since the age of 15, when I used to carry the WNPS edition in three volumes in a big rucksack on my field trips. *The Handbook of the Mammals of the World* (HMW), published in nine volumes by Lynx Edicions, was very useful in bringing me up to date with taxonomic changes. Each volume lists thousands of technical papers. To look up papers that are relevant to Sri Lankan mammals, the volume by Asoka Yapa and Gamini Ratnavira is a good starting point.

Information on behaviour has been based on my field observations, W. W. A. Phillips and *The Behaviour Guide to African Mammals*, as many Asian species are shared with Africa. For behaviour of mammals in general and behavioural insights into species shared between Europe and Asia, *European Mammals: Evolution and Behaviour* is excellent. For identification of whales and dolphins *Whales, Dolphins and Seals: A Field Guide to the Marine Mammals of the World*, was invaluable and I have often taken a copy out to sea with me. See below for details of these publications.

BIBLIOGRAPHY

Anderson, R. C. & Alagiyawadu, A. 2019. Observations of cetaceans off southern Sri Lanka, April 2007–2013. J. *Cetacean Res. Manage* 20: 13–25.

Bernede, L. & Gamage, S. 2006. *A Guide to the Slender Lorises of Sri Lanka*. Primate Conservation Society of Sri Lanka, Colombo.

Dalebout, M. L., et. al. 2014. Resurrection of *Mesoplodon hotaula* Deraniyagala 1963: A new species of beaked whale in the tropical Indo-Pacific. *Marine Mammal Science* 30(3): 1081–1108.

de Silva Wijeyeratne, G. 2007. *Sri Lankan Wildlife*. Bradt Travel Guides, UK.

de Silva Wijeyeratne, G. 2008. Best for Blue. Is Sri Lanka the world's top spot for seeing Blue and Sperm Whales? May 2008. Open Release Article.

de Silva Wijeyeratne, G. 2008. The Gathering – a billion rupees of elephants. *Hi Magazine*. December 2008. Series 6, Vol. 5. 202–204.

de Silva Wijeyeratne, G. 2010. Kalpitiya joins Sri Lanka's whale spots. *Sunday Times Plus*. 7 March 2010. Features.

de Silva Wijeyeratne, G. 2011. How Sri Lanka was positioned as being best for Blue Whales. *Daily Mirror*. Colombo. 28 July 2011.

de Silva Wijeyeratne, G. 2012. Sri Lanka best chance for Sperm Whale super-pods. *Sunday Times*: Sri Lanka. *Sunday Times Plus*. 5 August 2012. Features.

de Silva Wijeyeratne, Gehan. 2013. *Wild Sri Lanka*. John Beaufoy Publishing, UK.

de Silva Wijeyeratne. G. 2019. Sailing in dangerous waters. *Sunday Times*: Sri Lanka. *Sunday Times Plus*. 3 November 2019.

de Vos, A. 2017. First record of Omura's Whale, *Balaenoptera omurai*, in Sri Lankan waters. Mar *Biodivers Rec* 10, 18.

Dissanayake, R. 2012. The Nilgiri striped squirrel (*Funambulus sublineatus*) and the dusky striped squirrel (*Funambulus obscurus*), two additions to the endemic mammal fauna of India and Sri Lanka. *Small Mammal Mail* 3(2): 6–7.

Dissanayake, R. & Oshida, T. 2012. The systematics of the dusky striped squirrel, *Funambulus sublineatus* (Waterhouse, 1838) (Rodentia: Sciuridae) and its relationships to Layard's squirrel, *Funambulus layardi* Blyth, 1849. *Journal of Natural History*, 46:1–2, 91–116.

Duff, A. & Lawson, A. 2004. *Mammals of the World: A Checklist*. A&C Black Publishers Ltd, and Yale University Press.

Estes, R. D. 1991. *The Behavior Guide to African Mammals Including Hoofed Mammals, Carnivores, Primates*. Drawings by Daniel Otte. Russel Friedman Books, South Africa.

Gemmell, G. L., McInnes, J. D., Heinrichs, S. J. & de Silva Wijeyeratne, G. 2015. Killer Whale (*Orcinus orca*) Predation on whales in Sri Lankan waters. *Aquatic Mammals 2015*, 41(3), 265–271.

Groves, C. P. & Meijaard, E. 2005. Interspecific variation in *Moschiola*, the Indian chevrotain, in Contributions to biodiversity exploration in Sri Lanka, *The Raffles Bulletin of Zoology 2005*, Supplement

No. 12. National University of Singapore.

Groves, C. P., Rajapaksha, C. & Manemandra-arachchi, K. 2009. The taxonomy of the endemic golden palm civet of Sri Lanka. *Zoological Journal of the Linnean Society* 2009, 155, 238–251.

Ilangakoon, A. 2002. *Whales & Dolphins Sri Lanka.* WHT Publications (Private) Ltd. Colombo. Photographs and drawings. Illustrations by Prasanna Weerakkody.

Macdonald, D. 1995. *European Mammals: Evolution and Behaviour.* HarperCollins: London. Illustrated by Priscilla Barrett.

Martenstyn, H. 2018, 2nd edn *Out of the Blue.* Published by the author. Colombo, Sri Lanka.

Meegaskumbura, S., Meegaskumbura, M., Pethiyagoda, R., Manamendra-Arachchi, K. & Schneider, C. J. 2007. *Crocidura hikmiya,* a new shrew (Mammalia: Soricomorpha: Soricidae) from Sri Lanka. *Zootaxa* 1665: 19–30.

Meegaskumbura, S. & Schneider, C. J. 2008. A taxonomic evaluation of the shrew *Suncus montanus* (Soricidae: Crocidurinae) of Sri Lanka and India. *Ceylon Journal of Science (Bio. Sci.)* 37 (2): 129–136.

Meegaskumbura, S., Meegaskumbura, M. & Schneider, C. J. 2012. Phylogenetic position of *Suncus fellowesgordoni* with pigmy shrews from Madagascar and Southeast Asia inferred from cytochrome-b. *Ceylon Journal of Science (Bio. Sci.)* 41 (1): 83–87.

Meegaskumbura, S., Meegaskumbura, M. & Schneider C. J. 2012. Re-evaluation of the phylogenetic position of *Suncus fellowesgordoni* and its phylogenetic relationship with *S. etruscus.* *Zootaxa* 3187: 57–68.

Mittermeier, R. A., Rylands, A. B. & Wilson, D. E. (eds). 2013. *Handbook of the Mammals of the World. Vol. 3. Primates.* Lynx Edicions: Barcelona.

Phillips, W. W. A. 1980 (2nd rev. edn). *Manual of the Mammals of Sri Lanka.* Wildlife and Nature Protection Society of Sri Lanka, Colombo.

Shirihai, H. & Jarrett, B. 2006. *Whales, Dolphins and Seals. A Field Guide to the Marine Mammals of the World.* A&C Black Publishers: London.

Veron, G., Patou, M.-L., Toth, M., Goonatilake, M. & Jennings, A.P. 2015. How many species of *Paradoxurus* civets are there? New insights from India and Sri Lanka. *Journal of Zoological Systematics and Evolutionary Research* 53: 161–174.

Wilson, D. E. & Mittermeier, R. A. (eds). 2009. *Handbook of the Mammals of the World. Vol. 1. Carnivores.* Lynx Edicions: Barcelona.

Wilson, D. E. & Mittermeier, R. A. (eds). 2011. *Handbook of the Mammals of the World. Vol. 2. Hoofed Mammals.* Lynx Edicions: Barcelona.

Wilson, D. E. & Mittermeier, R. A. (eds). 2014. *Handbook of the Mammals of the World. Vol. 4. Sea Mammals.* Lynx Edicions, Barcelona.

Yapa, A. & Ratnavira, G. 2013. *The Mammals of Sri Lanka.* Field Ornithology Group of Sri Lanka.

Yapa, W. 2017. *A Field Guide to the Bats of Sri Lanka.* Dilmah Ceylon Tea Company PLC.

PHOTOGRAPHIC NOTES

The majority of photographs by me were taken in the wild. For a few species, especially nocturnal mammals, I used photographs of captive animals, mainly in the Colombo Zoological Gardens. Many of the small mammal images sourced from other photographers were also taken in captivity in zoos, or in the field during scientific projects when small mammals were being captured for study and/or tagging and released under a research permit. Many of the images of bats and very small mammals were taken by researchers working under permits in Sri Lanka or overseas. Researchers must obtain inoculations and be trained in handling mammals and having the right equipment, including gloves that minimize the risk of diseases being transmitted through bites. Furthermore, animal welfare is very important. Small mammals have a high metabolic rate and if mammal traps are not inspected frequently, with animals released soon after capture, they may die. Bat colonies are easily disturbed by people visiting caves; the presence of people sometimes changing the temperature, and humidity disturbing a colony. Wildlife photographers should remember that the welfare of the animal comes first. For authors like me, sourcing images from others is both time efficient and minimizes disturbance to vulnerable small mammals. I am grateful to everyone who shared their images.

GENERAL ACKNOWLEDGEMENTS

Many people have over the years helped me in one way or another to become better acquainted with Sri Lanka's natural history. My field work has also been supported by several hotels and tour companies, as well as state agencies and their staff. To all of them, I am grateful. I must, however, make a special mention of the corporate and field staff of Jetwing Eco Holidays (JEH) and its sister companies Jetwing Hotels and Jetwing Travels. During my 11 years of residence as a working adult in Sri Lanka, they hugely supported my efforts to draw attention to Sri Lanka as being super-rich in wildlife. In the corporate team, Hiran Cooray, Shiromal Cooray, Ruan Samarasinha, Raju Arasaratnam, Sanjiva Gautamadasa and Lalin de Mel and many others have supported my efforts. Past and present Jetwing Eco Holidays staff and Jetwing naturalists including Chandrika Maelge, Amila Salgado, Ajanthan Shantiratnam, Paramie Perera, Nadeeshani Attanayake, Ganganath Weerasinghe, Riaz Cader, Ayanthi Samarajewa, Shehani Seneviratne, Aruni Hewage, Divya Martyn, L. S. de S Gunasekera, Chadraguptha Wickremesekera ('Wicky'), Supurna Hettiarachchi ('Loku Hetti'), Suchithra Hettiarachchi ('Podi Hetti'), Chaminda Jayaweera, Sam Caseer, Chandra Jayawardana, Nadeera Weerasinghe, Anoma Alagiyawadu, Hasantha Lokugamage ('Basha'), Wijaya Bandara, Nilantha Kodithuwakku, Dithya Angammana, Lal de Silva, Chaminda Jayasekera and various interns have helped me. Chandrika Maelge, in addition to running the Jetwing Eco Holidays team, used her artistic and book-design skills to produce literature to brand Sri Lanka for wildlife as well as to develop simple pictorial guides to build identification skills, which are available online on the JEH website.

My late Uncle Dodwell de Silva took me on leopard safaris at the age of three and got me interested in birds. My late Aunt Vijitha de Silva and my sister Manouri got me my first cameras. My late parents Lakshmi and Dalton provided a lot of encouragement. My sisters Indira, Manouri, Janani, Rukshan, Dileeni and Yasmin and brother Suraj also encouraged my pursuit of natural history. In the UK, my sister Indira and her family always provided a home when I was bridging islands. Dushy and Marnie Ranetunge helped my return to the UK. My one-time neighbour Azly Nazeem, a group of then schoolboys including Jeevan William, Senaka Jayasuriya and Lester Perera, my former scout master Mr Lokanathan, and the late George Ondaatjie, an A Level Physics teacher, were key influences in my school days.

My development as a writer is owed to many people. Firstly, my mother Lakshmi and more lately various editors and their colleagues, including the team at *Lanka Monthly Digest*, *Living*, the *Sunday Times* and *Hi Magazine*, who encouraged me to write. At the risk of mentioning just a few, editors in print media who have supported my work in Sri Lanka include Hiran Hewavisenti, Renuka Sadanandan, Shyamalee Tudawe, Ifham Raji, Roy Silva and Marianne David. Various TV crews, especially the teams led by Asantha Sirimane at Vanguard and YATV, supported my efforts to popularize wildlife. My development as a naturalist has benefited from the programme of events organized by the Wildlife and Nature Protection Society, Field Ornithology Group of Sri Lanka (FOGSL) and Sri Lanka Natural History Society. In the UK, I have learnt a lot from the field meetings of the London Natural History Society and the London Wildlife Trust. I have also been fortunate to continue having good company in the field in Sri Lanka on my visits after I moved back to London. My friends and field companions include Ajith Ratnayaka, Nigel Forbes, Chitral Jayatilake and Ashan Seneviratne, who have arranged a number of field trips for me. Martin Wickremesinghe, who started a simple eco lodge in Sinharaja, has contributed hugely to the wildlife tourism industry and others such as myself by making available a comfortable and affordable base for field work.

My wife Nirma and two daughters Maya and Amali are part of the team. They put up with me not spending the time they deserve with them because I spend my private time working on the 'next book'.

Nirma, at times with help from parents the late Roland Silva and Neela Silva, takes care of many things, allowing me more time to spend on taking natural history to a wider audience. The list of people and organizations that have helped or influenced me is too long to mention individually, and the people mentioned here are only representative. My apologies to those whom I have not mentioned by name; your support did matter. Everything I know is what I have learnt from someone else.

SPECIFIC ACKNOWLEDGEMENTS

Various people helped with information generally or on specific topics. These include the late Ravi Samarasinha, Rukshan Jayewardene, Andrew Kittle and Anjali Watson on leopards, Anna Nekaris and Lilia Bernede on primates, especially lorises and nocturnal observation techniques, Shyamala Ratnayake (Sloth Bear), Charles Anderson (cetaceans), Georgina Gemmell (Orca), Anya Ratnayaka (Fishing Cat), Rohan Pethiyagoda and Suyama Meegaskumbura (small mammals), Rajith Dissanayake (squirrels), Rohit Chakravarty (bats) and Susannah Clarendon (cetaceans).

My first photographic guide to the mammals of Sri Lanka remains in print with Bloomsbury, and where species are common to both, the reader will find that some of the material is shared. However, there are many differences between the two books. I suspect some people may wish to have both.

The section on whales and dolphins draws heavily on the many hours I have spent at sea when I began a media blitz in May 2008 that Sri Lanka was the best for the Blue Whale. Many of those who supported my marine mammal field work are acknowledged more fully in the 37 articles I have written. I have to repeat my thanks to Mirissa Water Sports, Dallas Martenstyn and his investors at Barr Reef, and Jetwing Hotel for hosting me, together with the many media personnel I brought from the print and television media. The ensuing stories and media coverage helped to draw attention to Sri Lanka and resulted in those studying cetaceans in Sri Lanka being involved with the international media.

Tara Wikramanayake once again assisted with preliminary rounds of copy editing and posing questions. My thanks again to John Beaufoy and Rosemary Wilkinson for asking me to take on another book, and to Krystyna Mayer for her expert editing.

PICTURE CREDITS

I would like to thank all the photographers who contributed images. They are individually credited with the images they provided. Rohan Pethiyagoda, Susannah Clarendon, Ray Heaton, Nayer Youakim, John Beaufoy, Bikram Grewal, Rohit Chakravarty, Andy Swash and Asoka Yapa very kindly introduced me to various photographers to help me to source images. Thilani Rathnayake at Jetwing Safari Camp Yala assisted with queries when I was sourcing images. I am pleased that many of Sri Lanka's leading photographers, especially those specializing in small mammals, have contributed images. If I did not contact you for this edition but you would like to contribute images for the next one, please contact me on gehan.desilva.w@gmail.com.

Many images in this book could be improved upon in future editions. Books like this are a good way to showcase your work by being published by an international publisher and to have your images put to practical use. Many local and foreign visitors gift copies of these affordable books to local guides, helping to build skills at a local level and align conservation with an economic agenda. Some of the species for which I would especially like to receive images are as follows: Sri Lanka Shrew *Suncus zeylanicus*, Chocolate Pipistrelle *Falsistrellus affinis*, Montane Golden Palm Civet *Paradoxurus montanus*, White-tailed Wood Rat *Cremnomys blanfordi* and Omura's Whale *Balaenoptera omurai*.

■ INDEX ■

Other guides to Sri Lankan wildlife by
Gehan de Silva Wijeyeratne

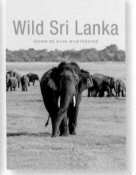